A DEVOTIONAL BIBLE STUDY
on THE BOOK *of* JAMES

Steadfast: A Devotional Bible Study on the Book of James

Published by The Gospel Coalition
2065 Half Day Road
Deerfield, Illinois 60015

Cover design: Gabriel Reyes-Ordeix

ISBN:
978-0-578-53342-1 (paperback)
978-1-7334585-1-1 (ebook)
978-1-7334585-0-4 (kindle)

Library of Congress Control Number: 2019915564

Printed in the United States of America

I can't wait to use this study of James with a group of women from my church! Courtney has put together well-worded questions that will help us think deeply about the text as well as keen insights and challenging applications.

—**NANCY GUTHRIE**, author and Bible teacher

Steadfast is an exceptional study that's easy to follow and allows for a deep dive into the book of James. Courtney Doctor not only guides us in our understanding of the text, she's written short prayers for every day as well as prompts to memorize Scripture. As we learn to ask the hard questions about our walk with the Lord and obedience to Christ, she reminds us that our steadfastness rests on his. I highly recommend *Steadfast* for personal or group study.

—**TRILLIA NEWBELL**, author of the study *If God Is for Us*, *Sacred Endurance*, and *God's Very Good Idea*.

Courtney Doctor's devotional Bible study on James has a theological depth, personal winsomeness, and practical value that sets it apart from ordinary devotional studies. Many of us know Courtney Doctor as a teacher who is both warm and deep. Those who study with her will see that those traits also manifest themselves in this God-honoring, disciple-making book.

—**DAN DORIANI**, professor of theology and VP of Covenant Theological Seminary

I am always looking for good bible studies for women in my church, and I love when I find one that drives women directly to the text of God's word. What I love even more is when the study also teaches them how to study the Bible for themselves. *Steadfast* does this very thing! By giving women the practical tools of Bible study (observation, interpretation, application, and reflection), Courtney Doctor doesn't just invite us to study with her, she gives us what we need to continue on with a lifetime of learning from God's Word no matter that text. This is a wonderful study for the women of your church, and I look forward to using it with my fellow sisters.

—COURTNEY REISSIG, Bible teacher and author of *Teach Me to Feel*

James compares hearing God's Word and not acting on it to looking in a mirror and forgetting what we have seen. Courtney Doctor's *Steadfast* devotional forced me to keep looking back at the text and not to forget or be unmoved by it. I saw new things in familiar texts and was changed. I recommend it highly.

—REBECCA MCLAUGHLIN, author of *Confronting Christianity: 12 Hard Questions for the World's Largest Religion*

So often when we study the Bible the foremost question in our minds is, "How does this apply to my life?" This is a valid question, and the book of James has a great deal of wisdom for Christian living. Yet, we don't do ourselves or our neighbors any favor if we rush to apply James's wisdom before we understand what he means. In this regard, Courtney Doctor has done us a great service. She lays out for us the right questions: what does the text say, what does it mean, how does it fit within all of Scripture, and how does it transform me? Moreover, she invites us to study and discuss in the most human way, in community. Take up this study. You will be encouraged and equipped for a steadfast life of following Jesus.

—IRWYN L. INCE, director of GraceDC Institute for Cross-Cultural Mission

Steadfast encourages women with practical biblical wisdom to walk out their faith in word and deed. It challenges women to thoughtfully examine whether the confession of their words matches their true possession of their hearts.

—**KAREN HODGE**, coordinator of women's ministries for the Presbyterian Church in America (PCA) and author of *Transformed: Life-taker to Life-giver* and *Life-giving Leadership*.

Dedication

◆

To Bo, Mickey, Ellis, and Patrick

May you each deeply know the steadfast love of the Lord and grow
into men of steadfast faith, full of the wisdom from above.
CC loves you!

*But the steadfast love of the Lord is from everlasting to everlasting
on those who fear him, and his righteousness to children's children.*
Psalm 103:17

Acknowledgements

◆

What a joy it's been to study the book of James and write this study! John Donne famously wrote that "no man is an island." I would add that no project stands alone, either. It would be impossible to acknowledge every person who has influenced my understanding of James, but please know that I'm grateful for the theologians, scholars, and godly saints who have given us all a rich collection of biblical insights. There are a few I would like to mention by name because their work has been particularly helpful to me for this study: Craig Blomberg and Mariam Kamell, Dan Doriani, Ralph Martin, Douglas Moo, and J. A. Motyer.

I'm deeply grateful to Melissa Kruger for asking me to write this study. Melissa, you bring so much wisdom, encouragement, and joy to a project. I'm grateful for your help, expertise, and, most of all, your friendship. Thank you to Winfree Brisley and Alyssa Miller; your editing skills and theological insights have made this a more clear and beautiful study. I've appreciated the fun and laughter along the way, too.

I owe a debt of gratitude to the women who willingly spent their summer working through the study and giving valuable feedback. Thank you, Caryl Wilson, for opening your beautiful home; Anna Porter for organizing; Bunny Hathaway and Sue Pitzer for leading discussions; and Rebecca Donaldson, Janet Tubbesing, Pat Kleinknecht, Anna Johnson, Carrie Spencer, Sharon Mason, Esther Bryan, Betsy Ziesness, Jodi Howell, Jennifer Spohr, Leah Jakes, and Sabrina Hickel for your time and thoughts. It was a joy to spend our Tuesday nights together!

I'm always grateful for my family, but I want to especially thank my daughters, Shelby and Rebecca. During your time at home this summer, you allowed me space to write when I needed it, but you also called me to close the computer when that was needed more.

Thank you for the practical ways you loved and helped, and the numerous ways you made me laugh! You bring deep joy to my soul.

To my husband and fellow writing buddy, Craig, thank you. Even in the midst of finishing your dissertation and numerous sermon preps, you willingly and cheerfully made umpteen grocery store runs, cooked at least as many dinners as I did, and were always willing to listen to me talk through a point I was wrestling with. Thank you for being a wise sounding board, a man of prayer, and a faithful friend.

My prayer is that the Lord would be pleased to take the labors, wisdom, gifts, and prayers that others have poured into this project, add to them the joy he's given me in writing it, and use it to build his church. May we, his bride, be conformed more to the image of our perfect Savior through this study.

Contents

◆

Introduction

◆

I always wanted to ride a school bus, but I was a carpool-kid. My mom regularly drove our neighborhood carpool in her mustard yellow station wagon with wood paneling down the side. The best part of that car was the seat in the rear that faced backwards. Everyone wanted to ride in that seat so we could wave and make faces at the people in the car behind us at the stoplight. Charming, I know.

The drive home from school was always interesting. Everyone would give a report on their day, which typically included some drama, a bit of tattling, victories, some frustrations, hurt feelings, and lots of questions—always lots of questions. My mom was somehow able to address the vast majority of topics and concerns being aired. She would jump from topic to topic, shooting arrows of advice into the variety of situations needing her wisdom.

"George, you ought to let Tim borrow your tennis shoes. You have an extra pair and it's the right thing to do."

"Kelly, I'm proud you got the highest grade, but how do you think it made Ellie feel when you told her, knowing she didn't do as well?"

"Courtney, I'm sorry you didn't get invited to Janie's slumber party. But that doesn't mean you should uninvite her from yours."

"Susan, I know spelling is hard for you. But I'm so proud of how you're sticking with it even though it takes you extra time."

"Mark, I understand your feelings were hurt, but that doesn't make your unkind words back to your sister okay. They're still wrong."

And on. And on. And on. These arrows of advice were my mom's attempts at speaking into the very real struggles we were facing. Her instruction was practical, spoken in love, and meant to help us do the right thing.

Reading James can feel like we're buckled in the backseat of his station wagon, on a five-chapter ride, with arrows of advice aimed right at us. Like the wisdom offered during my carpool rides, James is extremely practical. He meets us in the routine moments of our day. He meets us in our suffering, our illness, and our poverty. He confronts us in our speech, our wealth, and our pride. He instructs us when we lack the wisdom to know what to do next. James speaks into these very real, daily struggles by offering short commands (more than half of the 108 verses in the letter are commands!) on how one should live. Or, I should say, how a Christian should live.

James is speaking primarily to Christians—those who have already been given saving faith in Jesus. So, the commands given are not informing unbelievers about how they will earn God's favor or receive salvation if-and-when they obey the commands. No! James is first and foremost telling believers that they will, as a *result* of their true faith, live lives that reflect the salvation that is already theirs in Christ. Obedience does not earn God's love and acceptance; it's a result of the love and acceptance already ours.

Our response as we read, study, and apply the book of James should be two-fold. First, as we look honestly in the mirror James holds up, we are to ask ourselves if we're only hearers of God's Word or if we are, in fact, doers of it (1:22). James is concerned with how Christians live out their faith. We're to ask questions such as: Is my life characterized by living works of faith? Do my actions, words, and works reflect what I profess to believe? Do I do the good I know I should be doing? Am I humble? Do I love others the way I should? Am I steadfast in prayer?

As the answers to those questions become clear, we realize we don't (and can't) do all the Lord requires us to do. We try to obey and repeatedly fail. We strive to live up to the standards James has set out and consistently fall short. As we try and fail however, we become increasingly aware of our need for Jesus—the One who was perfectly obedient in every way.

Therefore, our second response should be to rest in the finished and complete work of Christ—the One whose genuine faith, perfect obedience, and steadfastness through trials *has* earned our salvation. He is the One who was perfectly steadfast under trials (1:12); he is the One who perfectly kept the whole law (2:10); he is the One who has pure religion (1:27); he is the One who perfectly submitted himself to God (4:7); and he is the One who humbled himself and whom God exalted (4:10). Studying James should make us long for and love the good news of the gospel of Jesus Christ: that we belong—body, mind, and soul—to our faithful Savior.

May our study of the book of James cause us to overflow with praise to the One who perfectly did everything the law commands. May our living hope in Jesus compel us to pursue faithful, steadfast obedience in every aspect of our lives as a result of our living faith.

WHAT TO EXPECT

◆

In this study, we want to not only glean the truths God has for us in the book of James, but also continue learning and applying good Bible study techniques. We'll do this by moving through the sequence of observation, interpretation, and application for each week's passage, over the course of five days of study.

Day 1 will always be *observation*—reading the passage and asking the question, *What does the text say?* Day 1 will involve slowly reading the passage several times, looking for patterns, repeated words, and key phrases. You may come up with several questions about the text as you read. This is great! Write them in the margins and see if you can answer them by the end of the week.

Day 2 will always be *interpretation part one*. We'll start asking questions of the passage like, *What does it mean?* We'll consider the context of the passage as we begin to interpret it.

Part of good interpretation involves looking at the whole counsel of God's Word, so Day 3 will be *interpretation part two*. We want to look at other relevant and related passages in Scripture and ask the question, *What do other Scriptures say?* On this day, you'll be looking up passages in both the Old Testament and the New Testament, in order to see how Scripture helps interpret Scripture. In the interest of time, some passages will be provided for you.

On Day 4 we'll be ready for *application*. We'll ask the question, *How does this text transform me?* We want to pay attention to what this passage teaches us about God and ourselves: what God has done and what we are to do in response. You'll have opportunities to respond in several ways.

Each week will end on Day 5 with a *reflection*. After reading it, you'll be asked to summarize what you've learned that week.

Please plan on approximately 30 minutes of study each day or 2.5 hours each week. Each day will begin with prayer—a time for you to ask God to meet you as you study his living and active Word. Even though the text for every week is provided for you to mark, comment, ask questions, and make observations on—I encourage you to have an actual Bible in front of you, rather than using an app on your phone or computer. You'll need it for cross-referencing verses and it helps you see the passage in its context more readily. The provided texts are from the English Standard Version, but use whichever translation you prefer.

MEMORY WORK:

A memory verse is provided each week. Spend a few minutes each day working on memorizing it. The discipline of hiding God's Word in your heart is one that will bear much fruit in your own life and the lives of those around you. At the end of the study, there is a "quiz" for you to see how many you can remember!

SMALL GROUP DISCUSSION:

At the end of each week (five days of study), you'll find a list of small group discussion questions. Ideally, you will be studying this book with others. We're created and designed to learn and grow best in the context of community. If you don't have others to study with, I encourage you to reach out and invite some! These questions are meant to help facilitate that learning and growth. There is a fun "icebreaker" question and a "warm-up" question—both are intended to be a quick, easy, and fun way to get the group going. Keep the answers to these short! The ten questions for small group discussion are where you will want to spend the majority of your time together. Don't feel the need to get through all of them, but pick and choose which questions best suit your group.

VIDEOS:

After June 2020, you will be able to access the keynote teaching sessions from TGCW20 online. Each keynote will feature a different Bible teacher teaching a passage in James and will align with the chapters in this study. These will be available at https://www. thegospelcoalition.org/conference/tgcw20/

May the Lord richly bless you with the presence of his Spirit, insight into his Word, more love for his Son, and greater conformity to his holiness.

CHAPTER 1

Steadfast Foundation: Our God of Perfect Gifts

◆

JAMES 1:1–18

(1) James, a servant of God and of the Lord Jesus Christ, To the twelve tribes in the Dispersion: Greetings.

(2) Count it all joy, my brothers*, when you meet trials of various kinds, (3) for you know that the testing of your faith produces steadfastness. (4) And let steadfastness have its full effect, that you may be perfect and complete, lacking in nothing.

(5) If any of you lacks wisdom, let him ask God, who gives generously to all without reproach, and it will be given him. (6) But let him ask in faith, with no doubting, for the one who doubts is like a wave of the sea that is driven and tossed by the wind. (7) For that person must not suppose

that he will receive anything from the Lord; (8) he is a double-minded man, unstable in all his ways.

(9) Let the lowly brother* boast in his exaltation, (10) and the rich in his humiliation, because like a flower of the grass he will pass away. (11) For the sun rises with its scorching heat and withers the grass; its flower falls, and its beauty perishes. So also will the rich man fade away in the midst of his pursuits.

(12) Blessed is the man who remains steadfast under trial, for when he has stood the test he will receive the crown of life, which God has promised to those who love him. (13) Let no one say when he is tempted, "I am being tempted by God," for God cannot be tempted with evil, and he himself tempts no one. (14) But each person is tempted when he is lured and enticed by his own desire. (15) Then desire when it has conceived gives birth to sin, and sin when it is fully grown brings forth death.

(16) Do not be deceived, my beloved brothers. (17) Every good gift and every perfect gift is from above, coming down from the Father of lights, with whom there is no variation

or shadow due to change. (18) Of his own will he brought us forth by the word of truth, that we should be a kind of firstfruits of his creatures.

* Or "brothers and sisters." The Greek word *adelphoi* is plural and can refer to both men and women who are siblings in the spiritual family of God.

DAY 1

Observation: What Does the Text Say?

◆

PRAY

Father, thank you for your living Word. As we come before it, help us to sit under its authority. We ask that you would open our eyes to see your glory and steadfast love in new ways as we study James. Help us see Jesus as the revelation of your wisdom and the true, perfect gift from above. And, Father, send your Spirit to instruct, convict, rebuke, train, nourish, and encourage us with your life-giving Word. In Jesus's name I pray. Amen.

READ JAMES 1:1–18

Today we're simply going to spend time observing the text—which means we'll read it several times (if possible, read it out loud), and ask questions about what we see. Good observation should always be the first step when we study any passage. Remember, James tends to move quickly from one topic to another. We'll follow his lead to glean the wisdom he has for us.

1. Go back through the provided text:

    a. Mark any words or phrases that stand out to you. Make note of patterns, key phrases, and repeated words.

    b. Write in the margin two to three things that stand out or questions you might have.

2. Who wrote the letter and how does he describe himself? To whom was he writing?

As you answer this question, you may feel like you're already a little lost in the book of James! It's helpful to know that the book of James is most likely the first New Testament letter written.[1] James is writing to the very first Christians, primarily Jews who have recently converted to Christianity. When he addresses them as "the twelve tribes in the Dispersion," he's using language that would be familiar to first-century Jews, but less familiar to us today.

Historically, the "twelve tribes" refer to twelve sons of Jacob, who formed the nation of Israel and were children of the promise given to Abraham (Gen. 15). The "dispersion" refers to Jews who remained scattered outside of the land of Israel after the exile (1 Chron. 9:1). James now uses these terms to highlight that the church is the true Israel, scattered throughout the world.

3. What does James command in verse 2? Why (verse 3)?

4. What does verse 2 tell us about the kinds of trials we will face? What do the words "when" and "various" teach us about these trials? In regard to trials, what is certain and what is variable?

5. Draw a diagram or image representing the relationship between trials, joy, knowledge, steadfastness, and completion (i.e. what comes first, what is/are the variable(s), what are the non-negotiables, and what is the result?).

Trials are a sure thing—everyone, everywhere, in all times will experience various trials. In some of Jesus's last words to his disciples,
he assured them of this very thing (John 16:33). Trials are certain,
but how we respond is not. James, knowing trials come to everyone, is first and foremost concerned with how we, as Christians,
respond to them. There's a response, he says, that will mature our
faith, strengthen our faith, and make us more like Christ. So, he exhorts us to respond well by being steadfast.

Steadfastness is crucial for the life of a believer. The Greek word
for steadfastness can be translated as patience (NKJV), endurance
(NLT), or perseverance (NIV). It indicates tenacity, grit, and deter-
mination. Steadfastness necessitates commitment and intentional
pursuit—nobody will be steadfast by accident. To be steadfast, as
we will see, is to be unwavering regardless of our circumstances.

The ultimate example of steadfastness is, of course, Jesus. The
author of Hebrews, using the same Greek word as James, tells us
that we are to run our races with endurance or steadfastness (Heb.
12:1). But the only way we can do that is by knowing the One who
went before us and ran his race with perfect steadfastness. He never
wavered and he intentionally, tenaciously, endured the cross. Hebrews 12:2 reminds us that Jesus was able to endure (be steadfast)
in his greatest trial by looking at the joy set before him; and we are
to endure by looking at Jesus, our greatest joy.

James tells us, that when we remain steadfast under trial, the
trial will have its intended outcome—we will become perfect and
complete. The phrase "to be perfect and complete" (James 1:4) refers more to spiritual maturity than moral perfection. Christians will
one day be made morally perfect, but not in this life. In this life, we
are to become increasingly like Jesus until that glorious day when
we actually *will* be like him (1 John 3:2). When trials come, and they
most certainly will, we're to look to Jesus; his steadfastness encourages and strengthens us in the midst of our trials. Those very trials

will produce in us that which will make us more like him—steadfast, able to endure.

6. What repeated root word do you see at the end of verse 4 and the beginning of verse 5?

7. What two words or phrases describe how God gives wisdom?

When James uses the word "faith" here, he's referring more to our confidence in God's character than in saving faith. James is talking to Christians, people already saved, so he's telling them to trust/believe/have faith that the God who saved them *through* faith will also give them the wisdom they need to *live out* that faith.

8. What two adjectives does James use to describe the doubter in verse 8? Contrast these two words with steadfastness.

9. What two kinds of people are described in verses 9–10? What are they each supposed to do? What is surprising or unexpected about this?

10. According to verse 12, who is blessed? When? What are they given?

11. Compare and contrast verses 2–4 with verse 12. What is similar and what is different?

12. Describe the two word pictures James uses to illustrate the connections between temptation, desire, sin, and death. What two things come together to conceive sin? What does sin produce?

13. In verses 12–15, we learn that God is not the giver of temptation. Instead, in verses 16–18, we're told God is the giver of what?

14. Fill in the blanks with the two words or phrases James uses to describe the steadfastness of God.

    a. There is no _____.

    b. There is no _____.

Each week we'll provide a verse from the study to memorize.[2] Take a few minutes today to work on the memory verse below. Try saying it out loud ten times in a row, each time looking at it less. Then, close your time in prayer, thanking God that every good and perfect gift is from above. Rejoice that he has given us the greatest gift of all—his one and only Son who, like his Father, is the same yesterday, today, and forever.

MEMORY VERSE

Every good gift and every perfect gift is from above, coming down from the Father of lights, with whom there is no variation or shadow due to change.

James 1:17

DAY 2

Interpretation: What Does the Text Mean?

◆

PRAY

Father, you have said that if any of us lacks wisdom, we can ask and you will give generously without reproach. I ask you for wisdom now, Lord. Please give me insight and understanding into your Word, that I might know it and obey it and be conformed to the image of Christ. In his name I pray. Amen.

READ JAMES 1:1–18

Most scholars agree that the James who wrote the letter we're studying was none other than the half-brother of Jesus, the biological son of Mary and Joseph! This means that he would have grown up with Jesus, possibly teased Jesus, maybe wrestled with Jesus. In tomorrow's homework we'll look at some verses that lead scholars to this conclusion. But today, think about what it might mean that James was the half-brother of our Lord.

1. What stands out to you about how James introduces himself in verse 1? How does he describe himself? What could he have said?

2. What do you notice about the way he refers to Jesus? Why do you think he does this?

3. Which of the two statements below more accurately restates what James says about joy in trials? What's the difference?

    a. Consider all of your circumstances as pure joy.

    b. Consider all of your circumstances with joy because God is at work in them.

4. Steadfastness could be described as . . . (list 3–4 words or phrases that could complete this sentence).

5. Why is steadfastness important in the life of a Christian?

6. One commentator stated that James "feared complacency more than persecution."[3] Why do you think this might be so?

7. Wisdom is the mark of a mature Christian. No wonder James tells us to ask for it! Why do you think we have to ask God for wisdom (as opposed to finding it in ourselves or elsewhere)?

8. What do you think it means to "ask in faith"? How is "asking in faith" the opposite of "doubting"?

9. Why is the illustration of a "wave of the sea" (verse 6) an accurate image of someone who doubts?

10. What two ways does James describe the doubter (verse 8)?

    a. Remind yourself of James's great hope for the believer. What is the word he uses (verses 3, 4, 12)?

    b. How are the words used in verse 8 to describe the doubter the opposite of how James hopes the Christian will respond to trials?

11. What do you think is the point of the illustration James uses in verses 10–11?

12. Who allows the *trials* in our lives and what is the intended outcome? Where do *temptations* come from and what is the intended outcome?

13. In verse 15, James says that "sin . . . brings forth death." According to verse 18, what does God bring forth?

Take a few minutes to work on the memory verse for the week. Try covering up some of the words and saying it without looking at them. Then, close your time in prayer, thanking God that he is the giver of every good and perfect gift.

MEMORY VERSE

Every good gift and every perfect gift is from above, coming down from the Father of lights, with whom there is no variation or shadow due to change.

James 1:17

DAY 3

Interpretation: What Do Other Scriptures Say?

◆

PRAY

Father, I bow before you and your living Word and ask that you would increase my love for both you and your Word. I confess that I don't always want to spend time studying it, and I ask that you would give me the desire to know you through your Word. I ask this in Jesus's name. Amen.

1.   Read the following verses. All of them record events prior to Jesus's death and resurrection. What do we learn about James in these verses?

MATTHEW 13:55	JOHN 7:3–5	MARK 3:20–21
Is not this the carpenter's son? Is not his mother called Mary? And are not his brothers James and Joseph and Simon and Judas?	So his brothers said to him, "Leave here and go to Judea, that your disciples also may see the works you are doing. For no one works in secret if he seeks to be known openly. If you do these things, show yourself to the world." For not even his brothers believed in him.	Then he went home, and the crowd gathered again, so that they could not even eat. And when his family heard it, they went out to seize him, for they were saying, "He is out of his mind."

2.   After the death and resurrection of Jesus, we see James become not only a follower of Jesus, but a leader in the early church (1 Cor. 15:3–8; Gal. 1:19; Acts 15:13–17). How does knowing this about James give you a deeper understanding of the significance of how James describes both himself and Jesus in James 1:1?

3. Make a list of words found in both James 1:2–4 and 1 Peter 1:6–8. In what ways did Peter expand on what James wrote?

JAMES 1:2–4	1 PETER 1:6–8
Count it all joy, my brothers, when you meet trials of various kinds, for you know that the testing of your faith produces steadfastness. And let steadfastness have its full effect, that you may be perfect and complete, lacking in nothing.	In this you rejoice, though now for a little while, if necessary, you have been grieved by various trials, so that the tested genuineness of your faith—more precious than gold that perishes though it is tested by fire—may be found to result in praise and glory and honor at the revelation of Jesus Christ. Though you have not seen him, you love him. Though you do not now see him, you believe in him and rejoice with joy that is inexpressible and filled with glory…

4. Read Romans 12:12. In what do we rejoice? How do these three commands work together?

I've heard wisdom described as the art or skill of godly living. Meaning, wisdom is the ability to take what you know to be true (based on knowledge, observation, and discernment) and apply it in a variety of circumstances, in a way that leads to godly living. James says we need wisdom, especially if we're to be steadfast in the midst of trials.

5. According to Proverbs 2:3–6, how are you to acquire wisdom? How does this compare to James 1:5–8?

6. Read 1 Kings 18:21 and Mark 12:29–30. How do these verses clarify what it means to be double-minded and why God is so opposed to such a person?

1 KINGS 18:21	MARK 12:29–30
And Elijah came near to all the people and said, "How long will you go limping between two different opinions? If the LORD is God, follow him; but if Baal, then follow him." And the people did not answer him a word.	Jesus answered, "The most important [commandment] is, 'Hear, O Israel: The Lord our God, the Lord is one. And you shall love the Lord your God with all your heart and with all your soul and with all your mind and with all your strength.'"

7. To ask in faith, without doubting, is to know, trust, and believe that God is good and faithful, and will give us all we need for life and godliness. According to Hebrews 11:6, why does the Lord want us to ask with faith and not doubt?

8. The wise man in Proverbs 30:8–9 says, "Remove far from me falsehood and lying; give me neither poverty nor riches; feed me with the food that is needful for me, lest I be full and deny

you and say, 'Who is the LORD?' or lest I be poor and steal and profane the name of my God."

a. What is the temptation in poverty, and what is the temptation in wealth?

b. What are we to desire instead?

c. How does James's description illuminate the unstableness of wealth? Why is wealth an insecure place to put our trust?

9. James highlights the brevity of life and wealth while reminding us of the blessing of remaining steadfast in both our trials and temptations. Thankfully, our steadfastness is rooted firmly in God's faithfulness. As Hebrews 10:23 reminds us, "Let us hold fast the confession of our hope without wavering, for he who promised is faithful." We can hold fast to God's ways in the midst of temptation because God is faithfully helping us at every moment. Read 1 Corinthians 10:13 and James 1:13–15. Com-

pare the path of the one who overcomes temptation to the one who falls into sin.

I CORINTHIANS 10:13	JAMES 1:13–15
No temptation has overtaken you that is not common to man. God is faithful, and he will not let you be tempted beyond your ability, but with the temptation he will also provide the way of escape, that you may be able to endure it.	Let no one say when he is tempted, "I am being tempted by God," for God cannot be tempted with evil, and he himself tempts no one. But each person is tempted when he is lured and enticed by his own desire. Then desire when it has conceived gives birth to sin, and sin when it is fully grown brings forth death.

a.   What do you learn about God from these two passages? What does he do and what does he not do?

b.   What do you learn about temptation and sin from these passages?

We can often believe our ability to fight temptation is the fruit of our own efforts and hard work. However, God is the true hero in our war against temptation. Yes, we have real choices to make, but we're only able to win the battle because God sets limits on our temptations and provides a way out so that we can endure. God is always acting on behalf of his children—every good and perfect gift is from him. Let's look at some verses that highlight the most important gift

God has given to those whom he loves. These truths are the foundation for every command he gives.

10. James 1:18 tells us, "Of his own will he brought us forth by the word of truth, that we should be a kind of firstfruits of his creatures." Read the following passages to help clarify what James is referring to in this verse.

    John 1:13: Who were born, not of blood nor of the will of the flesh nor of the will of man, but of God.

    Ephesians 1:13: In him you also, when you heard the word of truth, the gospel of your salvation, and believed in him, were sealed with the promised Holy Spirit.

    Ephesians 2:8: For by grace you have been saved through faith. And this is not your own doing; it is the gift of God.

    1 Peter 1:3: Blessed be the God and Father of our Lord Jesus Christ! According to his great mercy, he has caused us to be born again to a living hope through the resurrection of Jesus Christ from the dead.

    a. According to John 1:13, who willed your spiritual birth?

    b. According to Ephesians 1:13, what is the "word of truth"?

    c. According to Ephesians 2:8, what is the "gift of God"?

d.   According to 1 Peter 1:3, what attribute of God is listed as
     the reason we're born again?

e.   Write a sentence combining these truths.

Jesus is God's ultimate "good and perfect gift" that he sent down
from above. He is God's gift of grace, sent because of God's great
mercy. And it's through faith in the gospel (or good news) of Jesus
Christ that we are brought forth (or born again) into a living hope.
It's not because of our own doing, but is the gift of our good, good
Father. If you have received this good gift, use these truths to write
out a prayer of praise to God for your salvation. If you have not yet
received this gift, ask God to give it to you. He gives generously to
all who ask.

MEMORY VERSE

*Every good gift and every perfect gift is from above,
coming down from the Father of lights, with whom
there is no variation or shadow due to change.*

James 1:17

DAY 4

Application: How Does the Text Transform Me?

♦

PRAY

Father, transform me by the renewing of my mind and conform me more and more to the image of your Son. Thank you for your living and active Word. Amen.

READ JAMES 1:1–18

1. What hope do verses 2–4 offer you, or someone you know, who is going through a trial? How could these verses be misunderstood or misapplied?

2. James tells us we'll face a variety of trials. List 1–2 trials you are facing and write a prayer asking God to 1) help you stand in the sure hope he is working all things together for good and 2) show you how you can remain steadfast in the midst of it.

3. It is extremely difficult to change the way we feel about something—so it is very encouraging that James does not tell us to *"feel joyful* when you meet trials of various kinds." Instead, he tells us to "count it all joy"—meaning, *think about* or *consider* what we know to be true about God and rejoice in the fact that God is doing something good in the midst of our heartache.

Write down 4–5 truths about God you can hold fast to in the midst of your trials.

4. James reminds us, "if any of you lacks wisdom, let him ask God" (verse 5a). Do you feel as if you're lacking wisdom for a particular trial or difficult circumstance you're facing? Write down the specifics of what you need wisdom for and then spend some time asking God to give you the wisdom you need. As you do this, ask him to give you the faith you need to trust him in all things, and not doubt.

5. As we will see in future weeks of study, James has a lot to say about money, poverty, and riches—so we will be returning to these themes again. While money is neither inherently good nor inherently bad, it's a source of temptation for most of us. Whether we're living in plenty or in want, it's tempting to trust in money for our security, rather than trusting in God. Whether you consider yourself to be poor or rich, reread verses 9–11 and consider the following questions.

    a. How do these verses challenge you?

    b. How do they help you?

c. How might poverty and riches relate to trials and temptations?

d. In what ways are you trusting in money for security in your own life? How could refocusing your gaze on eternal truths help you trust in the Lord in new ways?

6. In what ways does considering the brevity of life help you gain wisdom for how you want to live your life?

7. According to verses 14–15, sin is conceived when desire meets temptation. List some desires you might have that could make you susceptible to particular temptations. How do these verses offer correction and hope?

8. If you're currently on a sinful path, how do these verses provide a strong warning to you? What do you need to do to stop, repent, and get back on the path that leads to life? Pray and ask the Lord to help you—he gives generously to all who ask.

9. Using the chart below, write down 2–3 trials you might face, or have faced. Then fill in the chart with 1) a desire that could lead

to a temptation, 2) what that temptation might be, and finally
3) a truth that will keep you steadfast through that trial.

TRIAL	DESIRE	TEMPTATION	TRUTH
Ex. Financial Difficulty	Financial Security	Bitterness over God not giving me what I want.	God will provide all I need. "And my God will supply every need of yours according to his riches in glory in Christ Jesus" (Phil. 4:19)

James lays out two paths in this chapter. Both journeys begin with a
trial, but the paths diverge according to the response of the person.
The person who responds with steadfastness walks a path which
leads to life, both here (verse 4) and in eternity (verse 12). The person who responds with doubt and selfish desire heads down a destructive path, one that ultimately ends in death. In the same way
the father in Proverbs (4:10–19) pleads with his son to see the two
paths and choose life, James pleads with his readers to do the same.

Thankfully, Christ holds us fast in the midst of life's trials and
temptations. He's the anchor that holds firm, keeping us secure in

the storm. He's the strength we need when our faith is weak. Close your time today making a list of as many of the good and perfect gifts the Father has given you as you can call to mind. Then, read that list out loud and thank God for his unwavering, steadfast faithfulness!

MEMORY VERSE

Every good gift and every perfect gift is from above,
coming down from the Father of lights, with whom
there is no variation or shadow due to change.

James 1:17

DAY 5

Reflection

◆

Today is a beautiful autumn day, and as I look out my window, I can see the magnificent colors of the leaves changing. The temperatures are also changing—we began the week in the 80's and are ending it in the 40's. The days are changing and becoming shorter. My lawn is changing from green to brown, my closet is changing to reflect the change in temperature, and my weekly menu planning is changing to incorporate more soup and less grilling.

Change is inevitable. Styles change. Portfolios change. We experience changes in health, weight, and hair color. Our levels of contentment, maturity, and joy can change from day-to-day and season-to-season. Children grow and change; our parents age and change; *we* age and change!

Everything changes . . . or maybe I ought to say, everything *created* changes. Because there is One who never changes. The Lord spoke through the prophet Malachi and said, "For I the LORD do not change; therefore you, O children of Jacob, are not consumed" (Mal. 3:6). The author of Hebrews tells us, "Jesus Christ is the same yesterday and today and forever" (Heb. 13:8). Our God is the eternal, *unchanging*, creator God.

And this is good news! It's the unchangeability of God, the fact he never wavers, that allows James to say there is "no shadow due to change" in him . . . not even the slightest hint of change.

God's unchangeability also means, even when we waver, he doesn't—he remains faithful. As trials come our way and we respond in faith, he is faithful to cultivate maturity in us. As trials come our way and we lack wisdom, he is faithful to provide wisdom when we ask. And when trials come our way and we respond with selfish desires that lead to temptation and sin, God is still faithful; he provides either a way out, conviction, or an opportunity to repent and be forgiven. He is steadfastly faithful.

In all of this, though, I'm glad there's one thing that can and does change . . . us! As God works in us, transformation is possible. We can become increasingly steadfast and mature. James tells us that's actually the point of the trials that come our way. They're meant to change us and produce in us the glorious fruit of Christ's steadfast-likeness. So, consider the trials that come your way as joyful opportunities to encounter the steadfastness of God and be changed into a mature, unwavering follower of Christ.

1. Take five minutes to summarize what you've learned this week and then use those thoughts to journal and guide your prayer.

2. Try to write the memory verse for this week's chapter, without looking at it!

GROUP DISCUSSION QUESTIONS

◆

ICEBREAKER: Using 1–2 words, name some little thing in your life right now that is bringing you happiness or delight. (It could be a new book, new pair of earrings, or a new app on your phone!)

WARM-UP: When you think of the term joy, how is that different than happiness? What's something that brings you joy versus something that gives you happiness?

Have someone (or several people) read James 1:1–18 out loud.

1. As you consider the author of this book and who it's written to, how does that change how you read and interpret it? Why is it important that we understand this book is written to Christians?

2. Trials come in all shapes and sizes. The only guarantee is that they will come. How does knowing trials are a part of life help you when you face them? Why is it helpful to know that God is at work in the midst of your trials?

3. What does it mean to be perfect and complete, lacking in nothing? What does it not mean? (See Heb. 2:10)

4. Describe someone you know who has a steadfast faith. What makes their steadfastness stand out to you?

5. What does it look like to be joyful in trial, but also be able to share about the reality of the trial with others? (See 2 Cor. 1:8–11) Why is this important to be able to do?

6. In what ways are we tempted in the midst of trials? Why do times of hardship make resisting temptation that much more difficult?

7. What has helped you fight sin and temptation in your own life?

8. What are some truths about God that you cling to in the midst of difficulties?

9. How is the character of God the foundation of steadfastness in the life of the Christian?

10. What was one thing that stood out/convicted/encouraged/instructed you this week?

Steadfast Obedience: Not Hearers Only

◆

JAMES 1:19–2:13

(19) Know this, my beloved brothers*: let every person be quick to hear, slow to speak, slow to anger; (20) for the anger of man does not produce the righteousness of God. (21) Therefore put away all filthiness and rampant wickedness and receive with meekness the implanted word, which is able to save your souls.

(22) But be doers of the word, and not hearers only, deceiving yourselves. (23) For if anyone is a hearer of the word and not a doer, he is like a man who looks intently at his natural face in a mirror. (24) For he looks at himself and goes away and at once forgets what he was like. (25) But the one who looks into the perfect law, the law of liberty, and perseveres, being no hearer who forgets but a doer who acts, he will be blessed in his doing.

(26) If anyone thinks he is religious and does not bridle his tongue but deceives his heart, this person's religion is worthless. (27) Religion that is pure and undefiled before God the Father is this: to visit orphans and widows in their affliction, and to keep oneself unstained from the world.

(1) My brothers [and sisters], show no partiality as you hold the faith in our Lord Jesus Christ, the Lord of glory. (2) For if a man wearing a gold ring and fine clothing comes into your assembly, and a poor man in shabby clothing also comes in, (3) and if you pay attention to the one who wears the fine clothing and say, "You sit here in a good place," while you say to the poor man, "You stand over there," or, "Sit down at my feet," (4) have you not then made distinctions among yourselves and become judges with evil thoughts? (5) Listen, my beloved brothers [and sisters], has not God chosen those who are poor in the world to be rich in faith and heirs of the kingdom, which he has promised to those who love him? (6) But you have dishonored the poor man. Are not the rich the ones who oppress you, and the ones who drag you into court? (7) Are

they not the ones who blaspheme the honorable name by which you were called?

(8) If you really fulfill the royal law according to the Scripture, "You shall love your neighbor as yourself," you are doing well. (9) But if you show partiality, you are committing sin and are convicted by the law as transgressors. (10) For whoever keeps the whole law but fails in one point has become guilty of all of it. (11) For he who said, "Do not commit adultery," also said, "Do not murder." If you do not commit adultery but do murder, you have become a transgressor of the law. (12) So speak and so act as those who are to be judged under the law of liberty. (13) For judgment is without mercy to one who has shown no mercy. Mercy triumphs over judgment.

* Or "brothers and sisters." The Greek word *adelphoi* is plural and can refer to both men and women who are siblings in the spiritual family of God.

DAY 1

Observation: What Does the Text Say?

◆

PRAY

Father, I bow before you today and ask that you help me not only understand your Word, but also obey it. I pray I would not be a hearer only, but that hearing would result in doing. Use your Word this week to instruct, correct, and train me in righteous living—that my life would be more aligned with your will and your character. Thank you for giving us your Word, implanting it in the hearts of your people, and enabling us to obey it. Amen.

READ JAMES 1:19–2:13 (IF POSSIBLE, READ IT OUT LOUD.)

Just like last week, it may feel like James is coming at us with rapid fire advice. Thankfully, we have five days to read, meditate, and consider what this passage is teaching us. Today, we'll begin by observing the text, asking questions like *who, what, when, where, why,* and *how*.

1. Go back through the provided text:

    a. Mark any words or phrases that stand out to you. Make note of patterns, key phrases, and repeated words.

    b. Write in the margin two to three things that stand out or questions you might have.

You've probably heard (and maybe even said) some of these pithy maxims:

> *Put your money where your mouth is.*
> *Actions speak louder than words.*
> *Pretty is as pretty does.*
> *Don't talk the talk if you can't walk the walk.*

They're all basically saying the same thing: if there's a discrepancy between what I say and what I do, my actions will be more believable than my words.

In our passage this week, James helps us understand these concepts from a Christian perspective. Faith is a gift from God that is accompanied by action. If we've heard and believed the Word of God, then our lives will accurately, consistently, and increasingly reflect the One we profess to follow. How we work, speak, react, respond, interact, love, consider, and care for those around us matters. These works either negate or confirm the believability of our professed faith.

2. How does James address his readers? Why does this matter?

3. James talks a lot about words—both ours and God's. What do verses 21–25 tell us about how we're to interact with God's Word?

4. With what does James contrast the "anger of man"?

The righteousness James speaks about here refers to the idea of righteous living. One commentator translates this verse as, "for man's anger does not bring about the *righteous life* that God desires"[4] (italics added). The apostle Paul will write in later letters about the righteousness of Christ that is given to us by God as a gift and credited to us as ours.[5] It's this work of Christ that allows us to stand before a holy God. It's because we're so completely covered in the righteousness of Christ, that our holy God can look at us and declare us righteous! We do nothing to earn or produce that righteousness. It's a gift, given freely by our loving God.

But James is talking about a righteousness that we play a part in *producing*—a righteousness that's lived out of knowing we've been covered in perfect righteousness. James wants his readers to understand that our lives need to reflect that God has declared us righteous. There are things we can do (or not do) that will produce (or not produce) righteousness in our lives. Unrighteous anger, he says, will not help anyone produce a life characterized by the righteousness that's ours in Christ. In the verses we're looking at today, James is going to tell us what righteousness looks like, lived out.

5.   Last week we looked at what the phrase "word of truth" means. What phrase does James use in verse 21 that might mean the same thing?

6.   What does "the implanted word" do? How are we to receive it?

7.   In verse 6, James said that someone who doubts is like a "wave of the sea." In verses 23 and 24, what word picture does James use to describe someone who is only a hearer and not a doer?

Have you ever gone out to dinner, walked into the restroom, and looked in the mirror only to see that you have a big piece of spinach caught between your front teeth? Or looked in the mirror at work to see that your shirt was on inside out? I have! And I can guarantee you that as soon as I saw what the mirror revealed, I fixed the problem! I removed the spinach and turned the shirt right side out. Never in a million years would I have seen the problem, shrugged my shoulders, and walked away from the mirror without fixing what was wrong. Knowledge of the problem was not enough; I needed to do something about it.

James tells us that the law of God (or God's Word) is like a mirror. It reveals our flaws. And just like a bathroom mirror, the longer I spend peering, the more flaws I see. If I just glance and quickly look away, I'll miss the revelation of my sin. For the Word of God to reveal the things in us that need to be fixed, we have to spend time gazing into it: reading it, thinking about it, memorizing it, understanding it, and then applying it—or as James says, *doing it*.

8. What two ways does James describe the law in verse 25?

9. List the three marks of true religion (verses 26–27). Next to each one, write what you think it means.

10. What is the clear command in James 2:1?

The word translated as *partiality* or *favoritism* in James 2:1 literally means "to receive someone according to their face."[6] That's such an

accurate description of favoritism! We're all so prone to look not
only at someone's face, but at their entire outward appearance—
their clothes, speech, jewelry, hairstyle, age, skin color—and quickly
decide how we'll receive them, or even *if* we'll receive them. James
condemns this behavior.

11. In verses 2–3, by what were each of the two men judged and
    what was each given as a result?

12. How is Jesus described in verse 1?

    a. To whom are the people James is writing to giving glory?

    b. Who deserves to be given glory?

13. According to verse 5, what has God done? According to verse 6,
    what does James say his readers have done?

14. Write down the "royal law" (verse 8).

15. Who is the one that is "doing well" (verse 8)? Who is the one that is "committing sin" (verse 9)?

Spend time memorizing and meditating on our memory verse for this week. Ask the Lord to help you, as you look into the mirror of his perfect Word, not just to hear it, but to be a woman who does what it says. And thank him for his great mercy shown to us in Christ!

MEMORY VERSE

But be doers of the word, and not hearers only, deceiving yourselves.

James 1:22

DAY 2

Interpretation: What Does the Text Mean?

◆

PRAY

Father, I come to your Word desiring to know it *and* do it. Please forgive me for the times I make studying your Word something to check off my to-do list. Thank you that your Word is living and active and is the place I can meet you, hear you, and know you. Please give me the meekness needed to receive your Word and allow it to take root in my heart and produce righteous living in me. In Jesus's name I pray. Amen.

READ JAMES 1:19–2:13

James wants his readers to know that the Word of God is meant to change us. We're supposed to respond to what we see and hear in the Word. For this change to occur, James says we have to be humble as we receive the Word. Humility requires that we listen carefully, speak slowly, and aren't easily or quickly angered.

1.   What do you think James might mean when he says that the implanted word "is able to save your souls"?

2.   List the characteristics of the hearer-who-does and the hearer-who-doesn't (verses 22–25).

     a.   Hearer who does:

     b.   Hearer who doesn't:

     c.   How is being a doer of the Word different than just being busy?

3.   In what ways is the Word of God like a mirror?

4.   What do you think James means when he uses the word "reli-
     gion" or "religious"? What are some ways those words are used
     today that are probably not what James has in mind?

5.   Keeping in mind that James is talking specifically about peo-
     ple who are vulnerable because of their socioeconomic poverty,
     who might fall into the orphan and widow categories today?
     What is their affliction? What does it mean to visit them?

6.   Rewrite the scenario found in 2:2–3 using a setting you encoun-
     ter in your daily life—your church, neighborhood, home, etc.

In verses 1–7, James writes using first a hypothetical scenario (verses
2–3), then a historical reality (verses 4–7). Presumably, the church
he's writing to is made up of mostly the socioeconomically poor who
are currently facing persecution from wealthy unbelievers in their
community. Sadly, the believers in the church have been showing
preference and honor to the socioeconomically advantaged (the
"rich") and dishonor to the poor in their midst.

7.   James asks four rhetorical questions. Read them below and re-
     write them as statements:

a.   Verse 4: [H]ave you not then made distinctions among
     yourselves and become judges with evil thoughts?

b.   Verse 5: [H]as not God chosen those who are poor in the
     world to be rich in faith and heirs of the kingdom . . . ?

c.   Verse 6: Are not the rich the ones who oppress you, and the
     ones who drag you into court?

d.   Verse 7: Are they not the ones who blaspheme the honor-
     able name by which you were called?

These aren't blanket statements condemning broad categories of
people. James isn't saying that all poor people will be saved, nor is
he saying that all rich people are condemned. He is speaking into a
specific situation, at a specific time, to a specific group of people—a
situation in which the rich oppressed the poor, and the church
(equally in the wrong) gave preferential treatment to the rich. In
the Old Testament, whenever the poor are oppressed, marginalized,
and neglected, God condemns those actions because he values all
people. He sees the unseen and helps the helpless.

The message of salvation is to go out to everyone—old, young,
men, women, Jew, Greek, rich, and poor. James is not saying that
God only saves the poor—but he is saying that he cares greatly for
the poor. The poor can be on the margins of society and, as a result,

be at greater risk in many areas. And our God is a God who protects the weak, defends the defenseless, and provides for the poor. He wants his people to do the same.

8. How is partiality (verses 1–9) related to judgement (verses 10–13)? How does that help you understand James's statement, "Mercy triumphs over judgement"?

9. Why do you think James uses the phrase "royal law" to describe the Scripture verse he quotes in verse 8?

10. How would you summarize 2:1–13 in one or two sentences?

As you work on your memory verse today, ask the Lord to help you not just learn about his Word, but receive it with meekness and do what it says. Ask him to show you how to be a doer of his Word by valuing, loving, visiting, protecting, and caring for the poor.

MEMORY VERSE

But be doers of the word, and not hearers only, deceiving yourselves.

James 1:22

DAY 3

Interpretation: What Do Other Scriptures Say?

◆

PRAY

Father, thank you that your great mercy is new every morning. Thank you that you have given us your living, active Word. Show me how to be a doer of the Word as well as a hearer. Open my eyes to the ways I show partiality, extend preferential treatment, and lack mercy. Change me so that I love the people you love and am merciful to others because of your great mercy to me. I ask this in the name of Jesus. Amen.

READ JAMES 1:19–2:13

1. James, like the book of Proverbs, is full of practical wisdom. Proverbs 17:27–28 tells us, "Whoever restrains his words has knowledge, and he who has a cool spirit is a man of understanding. Even a fool who keeps silent is considered wise; when he closes his lips, he is deemed intelligent." Write down the similarities you see between Solomon's words and James's in 1:19–20.

2. Look up the following verses and write down everything we're told to "put off," "put away," or "put to death."

EPHESIANS 4:22–25, 31	
COLOSSIANS 3:5–9	
I PETER 2:1	

As followers of Christ, there are things we need to do away with, take off, and crucify. One of the beautiful things about the gospel, is that in Christ, we really are made new. The old has truly gone and we're made clean (2 Cor. 5:17). The Old Testament passages below highlight how the implanted word saves us and makes us new creations—which has been God's plan all along.

3. Read Jeremiah 31:33.

   a. Where does God put his law? How does he do it?

b.   What phrase in James 1:21 captures this truth?

4.   Read Ezekiel 36:25–27.

 a.   When God sprinkles clean water on us, what happens to us?

 b.   What does James call our "uncleannesses" in James 1:21?

 c.   What two things does God "put within us"?

 d.   When God gives us a new heart and writes his law upon it, what does he cause us to do? How does this relate to what James is talking about in 1:22?

5.   Both James and Jesus talk about the importance of not just hearing God's Word, but doing it, obeying it, putting it into practice. Read Matthew 7:24–27. Make a list of everything true about the hearer-who-does and the hearer-who-doesn't in Matthew 7:24–27.

 a.   Hearer who does:

b. Hearer who doesn't:

6. James says that bridling our tongues is a mark of true religion—
    and the inability to do so suggests our religion is worthless or
    empty. Read Matthew 15:18–19. Where does Jesus say our words
    originate? In what ways does this help us understand why
    James can say that our words are an indicator of the sincerity
    of our faith?

7. Read the following verses from the Old Testament and answer
    the question following the verse:

    Deuteronomy 10:17–18: For the LORD your God is God of gods
    and Lord of lords, the great, the mighty, and the awesome God,
    who is not partial and takes no bribe. He executes justice for the
    fatherless and the widow, and loves the sojourner, giving him
    food and clothing.

    a. What does God do for the fatherless and the widow?

    Deuteronomy 24:19: When you reap your harvest in your field
    and forget a sheaf in the field, you shall not go back to get it.
    It shall be for the sojourner, the fatherless, and the widow, that
    the LORD your God may bless you in all the work of your hands.

    b. What does God command his people to do for the father-
        less and the widow?

Psalm 68:5: Father of the fatherless and protector of widows is God in his holy habitation.

    c.   Who is God to the fatherless and the widow?

Isaiah 1:17: learn to do good; seek justice, correct oppression; bring justice to the fatherless, plead the widow's cause.

    d.   What does God want his people to do for the fatherless and the widow?

8.   How do Jesus's words in Matthew 25:35–40 give us a different perspective on visiting orphans and widows in their affliction?

After talking to his readers about caring for the orphan and the widow, James immediately moves into talking about showing no partiality. Why? Because these two things are intimately related!

9.   Read 1 Samuel 16:7 and Romans 2:11. How do these verses portray God in contrast to the people James is writing?

10.   Remember the royal law? It is to "love your neighbor as yourself" (2:8). With that in mind, read Luke 10:25–37.

    a.   What question did the lawyer ask in verse 29?

b. How does Jesus's answer tie together loving your neighbor and not showing partiality? (Note: Samaritans were looked down on by the Jews.)

11. Read Romans 13:9. Why do you think the "royal law" is the summation of all the commandments?

As you work on memorizing James 1:22, ask the Lord to show you the ways you might hear the Word but not do the Word. Ask him to give you concrete ways you can love your neighbors.

MEMORY VERSE

But be doers of the word, and not hearers only, deceiving yourselves.

James 1:22

DAY 4

Application: How Does the Text Transform Me?

◆

PRAY

Lord, I want to be like the wise man who heard your Word and put it into practice. I want to have my life built on the steadfast rock of Christ and his Word. Please use my time in study today to take your Word, plant it deep in my soul, cause me to walk in your ways, and make me steadfast in my obedience to you out of my great love for you. Amen.

READ JAMES 1:19–2:13

1. The speed at which we speak and listen can impact our anger in both positive and negative ways. How do you struggle with anger when you're slow to listen? How does being quick to speak in your anger lead you to say things you regret?

2. In what ways does being quick to speak and slow to listen overflow in harmful ways to those around you?

3. Go back to question two from "Day 3: Interpretation." Choose three things from the chart you would most like to *put away* or *put off* and write them below. Next to each, write a prayer asking the Lord to help you.

In 1:22, James says that if you and I are hearers only, we deceive ourselves. One commentator says the "idea of 'deceive' in [this] context
is clear: to be 'deceived' is to be blinded to the reality of one's true
religious state. People can think they're right with God when they
really are not."[7] Looking into the mirror of God's perfect Word is
important! We want to see if we've been deceiving ourselves about
the genuineness of our faith. We look and ask, "Have I only been
hearing God's Word and so deceiving myself, or am I truly someone
who obeys and does what he says?"

4.   As you looked into the perfect mirror of God's Word this week,
     what have you seen?

5.   How will you respond to what you've seen so you're not like
     the one who looks in the mirror and then forgets what she saw?

6.   James is clearly concerned that we not only hear the Word,
     but know it and do it. Note the specific way(s) you're current-
     ly living out the three marks of true religion . . . or a way you
     could begin to:

     a.   Bridling your tongue:

     b.   Caring for the fatherless and husbandless:

    c.   Keeping yourself unstained from the world:

It's extremely important to note, that these three marks are *evidence* of true faith, not the cause of it. Meaning, they're things we'll do as a result of the Word implanted in us. It's also not an exhaustive list of what the true believer does—it's a representative list. The person with genuine faith will do more than just bridle her tongue; she'll desire her words to accurately reflect her new heart. The person with genuine faith will do more than visit orphans and widows in their distress; she'll want her heart to be aligned with God's heart and to love whom he loves. And the person with true faith will do more than keep herself unstained from the world; she'll desire an increase in personal holiness in all areas of her life. All of this is a result of the Lord's saving work already accomplished in us.

The word "religion" can have a bad rap in our society for so many reasons. But James obviously thinks religion is a good thing. One commentator says this, "James says, in effect, 'Does the show of religion frighten you? A religion that never shows itself publicly frightens me.'"[8]

7.   Why is this distinction (of public religion) important?

Widows and orphans were some of the most vulnerable people in the ancient Near East. They were on the margins of society with little protection or provision because of their financial situation. But, as we just saw in the passages above, the Lord sees, loves, protects, defends, and provides for those on the margins of society. And he wants the hearts of his people to be aligned with his.

8. In what ways do you see, love, protect, defend, and provide for those on the margins of society today?

9. In what ways are these verses a mirror showing you something that needs to change? Remember, James implores us to not be hearers only, but doers who act!

The word James uses for "shabby clothes" is the same root word he used in 1:21 for "filthiness." We probably all know what it's like to stand next to someone who is literally "filthy." They can smell bad. Maybe their clothes are dirty, maybe they haven't bathed in a while . . . whatever the nature, their filth can make us want to move in the opposite direction. What James wants us to see is that we're all filthy! Filthiness is not just on us, but in us. And the amazing thing is that Jesus didn't move away, he moved near. He came to us in our "filthiness and rampant wickedness," showing no partiality, and he sat with us. We're the poor and the filthy. Praise be to God who has made the "poor in the world to be rich in faith and heirs of the kingdom" (James 2:5).

10. How does knowing that you are the "poor man in shabby clothing" change the way you think about not showing partiality?

11. We said on Day 1 that partiality could be described as receiving someone "based on their outward appearance—their clothes, speech, jewelry, hairstyle, age, skin color—and quickly deciding how we'll receive them, or even *if* we'll receive them." In what

ways do you struggle with making judgements about others based on their outward appearance?

    a.   Who are your neighbors that you're tempted to discriminate against, or who is difficult for you to love?

    b.   Is there a neighbor God is calling you to move towards? If so, write down the name(s) and ask him to give you the opportunity to visit them. If not, ask him to show you someone he wants you to move towards.

12. Where in your life does mercy need to triumph over judgement in a relationship with someone?

13. Make a list of the ways the Lord has been merciful to you. Spend some time in prayer thanking him for his mercy!

DAY 5

Reflection

◆

God is serious about mercy—his and ours. When Moses asked to see God, God chose to reveal himself by describing his character, and the first word he chose was *merciful*. "The Lord, the Lord, a God merciful and gracious" (Ex. 34:6). Mercy is a defining attribute of God. It's an attribute he wants his children to have too.

The first part of James 2:13 cannot be skipped over or taken lightly. James says that anyone who has not shown mercy to others—the poor, the fatherless, the widow, the oppressed, the neighbor—will be judged without mercy. We saw in the parable of the unmerciful and unforgiving servant, that God expects those who've received mercy to extend mercy.

Additionally, James gives us three things that are the test of true religion: bridling your tongue, visiting orphans and widows in their affliction, and keeping yourself unstained from the world. But as we ask God to use his Word as a mirror, we see that we fail at all three points. James also says that if anyone breaks God's law at even one point, she has broken the entire thing. Therefore, we know we can never be saved by our good deeds or by the law; we know we need mercy. And then we read that if we haven't shown mercy, we won't receive it! How are we to escape our predicament?

Throughout the Old Testament, God met with his people in the tabernacle (and eventually the temple). Once a year, and only once a year, the high priest made many sacrifices and much blood was shed. But after these things occurred, the high priest could enter the Most Holy Place and meet with God. In the middle of the Most Holy Place was the ark of the covenant. Inside the ark, were the two stone tablets with the law that the Lord had given to Moses on Mt. Sinai. But covering the ark and the law was the mercy seat. And it was on the mercy seat that the Lord told Moses he would meet with him (Ex. 25:17–22). The literal place the Lord met with his people was from a seat of mercy.

But now, we have full access to the Most Holy Place because of Jesus—our final high priest (Heb. 4:14), our perfect sacrifice (Heb. 10:12). And we are covered by his blood that was shed for us (Heb. 10:19). Jesus is the embodiment of God's mercy. It is *in Christ* that we find the mercy of God.

To be very clear, God's mercy only triumphs over his judgement for those who are *in Christ*. Conversely, judgment triumphs over mercy for anyone not in Christ. The reason is this: judgment and mercy met perfectly in Christ on the cross. Mercy did not triumph over judgement for Christ—he bore the judgement that was ours so he could extend the mercy we so desperately need. Justice was met, as mercy was given; both were on full display. Therefore, God will judge everyone according to who they are in Jesus—mercy for those found in him, and judgement for those not.

It's God's mercy in Christ that saves us. God knew we would never perfectly keep his law or fulfill the marks of true religion. We never earn or deserve God's mercy. We can't. But, as a result of his great mercy given in Christ, he calls us to show mercy to others who can never earn or deserve ours—the poor, the fatherless, the widow, the oppressed, the neighbor. In fact, he says if we don't show mercy to others, we have to question whether or not we've actually received his mercy. It's not that our merciful acts to others earn us God's mercy. It's that our merciful acts to others reveal that we've been the grateful recipients of a greater mercy—a mercy that will cover and triumph over judgement for those who are in Christ.

1. Take five minutes to summarize what you've learned this week and then use those thoughts to journal and guide your prayer.

2. Try to write the memory verse for this week's chapter, without looking at it!

GROUP DISCUSSION
QUESTIONS

◆

ICEBREAKER: Answering with just a word or a phrase, what's something you tend to forget?

WARM-UP: When you think of God showing mercy, what examples from the Bible or your own life come to mind?

Have someone (or several people) read James 1:19–2:13 out loud.

1. What are some practical ways we can be quicker to listen, slower to speak, and slower to anger?

2. Tell the group about a time you wished you had been slower to speak or quicker to listen.

3. What's the difference between being angry because you're right, and righteous anger? How could being slow to anger help restrain unrighteous anger?

4. What are the three marks of true religion that James gives? How do these compare to the ways we tend to evaluate our faith?

5. In what ways is it a false dichotomy to say that God cares more about our hearts than our actions? Why do you think God cares that we "walk the walk if we talk the talk" or, as James said it, that "we're doers of the word and not hearers only" (1:22)?

6. Why do you think we tend to show preferential treatment to the socio-economically advantaged but neglect the socioeconomically disadvantaged?

7. What might it look like to visit orphans and widows today?

8. How could we, as the church, do a better job of caring for the poor?

9. What did you see as you looked into the perfect mirror of God's Word this week? What are your plans to remember what you saw and do something about it?

10. What was one thing that stood out/convicted/encouraged/instructed you this week?

CHAPTER 3

Steadfast Works: By Faith Alone

◆

JAMES 2:14–26

(14) What good is it, my brothers*, if someone says he has faith but does not have works? Can that faith save him? (15) If a brother or sister is poorly clothed and lacking in daily food, (16) and one of you says to them, "Go in peace, be warmed and filled," without giving them the things needed for the body, what good is that? (17) So also faith by itself, if it does not have works, is dead.

(18) But someone will say, "You have faith and I have works." Show me your faith apart from your works, and I will show you my faith by my works. (19) You believe that God is one; you do well. Even the demons believe—and shudder! (20) Do you want to be shown, you foolish person, that faith apart from works is useless? (21) Was not Abraham our father justified by works when he offered up

his son Isaac on the altar? (22) You see that faith was active along with his works, and faith was completed by his works; (23) and the Scripture was fulfilled that says, "Abraham believed God, and it was counted to him as righteousness"—and he was called a friend of God. (24) You see that a person is justified by works and not by faith alone. (25) And in the same way was not also Rahab the prostitute justified by works when she received the messengers and sent them out by another way? (26) For as the body apart from the spirit is dead, so also faith apart from works is dead.

* Or "brothers and sisters." The Greek word *adelphoi* is plural and can refer to both men and women who are siblings in the spiritual family of God.

DAY 1

Observation: What Does the Text Say?

◆

PRAY

Father, I bow before you as I open your Word today. I confess that I add nothing to the free gift of my salvation, and I thank you that Christ accomplished everything needed to save me. I ask that you would, through my encounter with your living Word, show me if my works confirm the reality of my faith. Help me to display, through my works, what it looks like to be a woman saved by the grace of God. Amen.

READ JAMES 2:14–26 (IF POSSIBLE, READ IT OUT LOUD.)

Remember, today is the day we just observe the text and ask questions like *who, what, when, where, why,* and *how*.

1. Go back through the provided text:

    a. Mark any words or phrases that stand out to you. Make note of patterns, key phrases, and repeated words.

    b. Write in the margin two to three things that stand out or questions you might have.

Chances are, you wrote some big question marks next to a few of the verses we're studying this week. That's good! One commentator says that this week's passage in particular is "the most theologically significant, as well as the most controversial, in the Letter of James."[9]

We'll see why as we spend time in it. But let me warn you, we're not going to quickly resolve the tension we might feel. We're going to go slowly, let James speak, and then let the whole council of God's Word inform our understanding.

2.   Is James speaking to professing believers or unbelievers? How do you know?

3.   James begins the passage speaking of a hypothetical "someone." What does this person "say" or "claim" (NIV) he has and doesn't have (verse 14)?

4.   What is the big question James is asking at the end of verse 14? What answer does he expect?

These are important answers to remember as you study this week. James is talking to believers about someone who claims to have faith, most likely a person in their congregation. This person is a professing believer and the big question James wants this person to ask is, *Is my faith real?* It's a question every professing believer needs to ask. James is going to tell us how we can know the answer to that question.

5.   How would you describe the person mentioned in verse 15?

a.   Is this person a believer?

b.   How do you know?

6.   James asks the same question in verses 14 and 16—*what good is it*? Fill in the blanks below.

a.   Verse 14: What good is it if someone says he has _____ but does not have _____?

b.   Verse 16: What good is it if someone says _____ but does not _____ _____?

7.   What is the conclusion James arrives at in verse 17?

8.   In verse 18, James introduces a hypothetical "someone" with an opposing view. What two things does this person try to pit against each other? How does James connect these two things?

These verses are not about a contrast between faith and works. They're about a contrast between true faith and false faith. True faith is proved to be real because it results in good works. False faith is proved to be dead because it does not result in good works. Anyone can say that they believe in God, even demons (verse 19)! James is saying that a profession of faith will prove to be legitimate, saving faith by the things the professing person does. The faith that never results in good works is, in fact, not a real, true, saving faith.

9.   What does James say the demons believe and what do the demons do? (Some scholars think James is making the point that at least the demons *do* something.)

10.   James introduces two historical figures as witnesses for his argument. Who are they?

11.   When does James say Abraham was justified?

12.   James says that Abraham's faith was _____ along with his works and _____ by his works.

13.   When does James say Rahab was justified?

14. How many times in these verses does James mention faith without works? What words and phrases does he use to describe a faith without works?

Don't miss the point: James wants his readers to make sure their faith is real. It's the epitome of pastoral concern. He doesn't want his readers to just know things about God, or even be able to articulate truths about God—no, he wants to make sure his readers know God, having been saved by him!

As you spend time working on our memory verse for this week, ask the Lord to show you if, and how, your faith has resulted in good works.

MEMORY VERSE

But someone will say, "You have faith and I have works." Show me your faith apart from your works, and I will show you my faith by my works.

James 2:18

DAY 2

Interpretation: What Does the Text Mean?

◆

Father, I come to your living Word today and ask that you would use it as a mirror—show me if my deeds confirm the reality of my profession of faith. Use your Word to convict and instruct me so that my life will be more aligned to your perfect will. Amen.

READ JAMES 2:14–26

Sola is a Latin word meaning *alone*. We use that word to confess five foundational truths of our faith. They are:

- *Sola Scriptura* (Scripture alone)
- *Sola Fide* (faith alone)
- *Sola Gratia* (grace alone)
- *Sola Christus* (Christ alone)
- *Soli Deo Gloria* (to the glory of God alone)

As Christians, we believe that Scripture alone is the written revelation of God, that salvation is through faith alone, by grace alone, in Christ alone, and that we live for the glory of God alone.

But if those are true confessions, then what does James mean when he says that a "person is justified by works and *not by faith alone*" (verse 24, italics added)? One commentator answers in this way, "[James] approaches [his readers] with his challenging question, not because he would propose a different way of salvation, but because he would have them understand what 'by faith alone' really means."[10] That's what I hope we do in our study today!

1. James asks the question, "What good is it?" twice in three verses.

    a. The first time he asks it (verse 14), James suggests that a profession of _____ without deeds does the professing Christian no good.

    b. The second time he asks it (verse 16), James suggests that words without _____ do the poor person no good.

    c. What point do you think James is trying to make?

2. How significant is the word "says" or "claims" (NIV) in verse 14? Why?

    a. What's the difference between a person who does not profess faith and a person who claims to have faith but has no works?

    b.   What's the difference between a person who claims to have faith but has no works and a person who claims to have faith and has good works?

3.   Circle the description that you think best explains the phrase "poorly clothed" in verse 15:

    a.   "Not very stylish" or "Insufficient for the weather and elements"

    b.   How do you think the "poorly clothed" person in verse 15 differs from the person in "shabby clothes" we saw in verse 2?

    c.   What would a person with true faith have done in verse 16?

4.   What do you think James might mean by the word "dead" (verses 17 and 26)?

5.   Circle which of the following you think best represents James's understanding of the relationship between faith, works, and salvation[11] (the arrow means "results in"):

- Works = Salvation
- Faith + Works = Salvation
- Faith = Salvation
- Faith = Salvation + Works

6. Looking Back: How do verses 1:17–18 inform your choice above?

7. We said on Day 1 that James is not contrasting faith with works. What is he contrasting?

In verse 18, the hypothetical arguer says that one person can have faith and another person can have works . . . and both are valid. James rebukes him.

8. What could faith without works look like?

9. Conversely, what could works without faith look like?

James references two Old Testament witnesses—Abraham and Rahab. These two people could not be more opposite! Abraham was the father of the Jewish faith, the first patriarch, a wealthy, influential, esteemed, and powerful man (Gen. 12–25). Rahab was a Canaanite prostitute. She was a poor, ill-esteemed, and powerless woman (Josh. 2:6). Yet, James chooses these two, polar opposite people to prove his point—that our deeds show whether or not our faith is genuine.

10. Why do you think James might have chosen two such opposite people to make his point?

11. How is the analogy James uses in verse 26 a powerful illustration of what faith without works looks like to God?

12. In one sentence, how would you state the point James is making in this passage?

As we'll see in tomorrow's work, we *are* saved by faith alone—but true faith does not remain alone. The implanted word, which saves us, is meant to grow and produce fruit in us and through us. Meditate on your memory verse today, and ask the Lord to use his Word to produce the fruit of good works in your life.

MEMORY VERSE

But someone will say, "You have faith and I have works." Show me your faith apart from your works, and I will show you my faith by my works.

James 2:18

DAY 3

Interpretation: What Do Other Scriptures Say?

◆

PRAY

Father, I ask that your Word would accomplish your purposes in me today. Use your Word today to teach, rebuke, correct, and train me in righteous living. I ask that you would meet me as I study. Give me insight and understanding, and help me to apply what I learn. Thank you that your Word is life. Amen.

READ JAMES 2:14–26

Faith, works, and justification—James wasn't the only biblical author to write about how these three things are related. The writer of Hebrews, the apostle John, and the apostle Paul (just to name a few) all wrote about the connection between faith, works, and justification.

Many scholars have noted that, on the surface, it looks as if James and Paul might disagree. Paul said that Abraham was not justified by works, but by faith (Rom. 4:2–3). James says that Abraham was justified by what he *did* and that a person is not justified by faith alone, but by works. So which one is it? Is James right or is Paul right? As we take a closer look, we'll see that they're both right—and that they couldn't agree more!

Let's begin by looking at the different ways two of these words can be defined and used.

Works:

- Paul talks a lot about *pre-salvation* works. He makes it clear that salvation is never earned through works or good deeds.
- James talks more about *post-salvation* works. He makes it clear that salvation always results in works and good deeds.

Justified:

- Justification is the act of being *declared* righteous by God.
- It also means being *proven* righteous through the *demonstration* of righteousness, or in other words, our actions showing/proving that we have been declared righteous.

1. Read Galatians 2:16.

    a. Who wrote Galatians?

    b. Fill in the blanks: A person is not _____ by _____ but through _____ in Jesus Christ.

c. Why do you think the phrase "works of the law" might be significant?

2. Read Ephesians 2:8–10.

a. How many times does Paul use the word "works"?

b. Using the "works" and "justified" definitions from today's introduction, which meaning do you think Paul was using in verse 9?

c. Which meaning do you think Paul was using in verse 10? What word does Paul use to describe these works?

d. How does this passage help you interpret James 2:24?

3. Read Romans 3:21–24 below. Underline the word "righteousness."

But now the righteousness of God has been manifested apart from the law, although the Law and the Prophets bear witness to it—the righteousness of God through faith in Jesus Christ for all who believe. For there is no distinction: for all have sinned and fall short of the glory of God, and are justified by his grace as a gift, through the redemption that is in Christ Jesus.

    a.   Who does Paul say the righteousness of God is for?

    b.   How do people receive righteousness?

4.   Read Matthew 25:31–46.

    a.   Who is telling the parable?

    b.   Using the definitions above, what kind of works is he talking about?

    c.   What similarities do you see between the works mentioned in the parable and the works James talks about?

5.   Read 1 John 3:17–18.

    a.   What question does John ask?

b.   What is John's concern in this passage?

c.   What similarities do you see between this verse and James 2:14–16?

Have you ever heard someone say, "Timing is everything"? It's particularly true in this conversation about faith, works, and justification. The key to understanding the relationship between works and faith is to identify the timing of the works. Are they pre- or post-salvation? Paul seems to be addressing the person who thinks that good works will save her—pre-salvation works. James seems to be addressing the person who professes faith, but never produces the fruit of good works—post-salvation works. Works aren't the root of salvation, they're the fruit of salvation; they're not the cause, they're the result. Understanding this will help us understand what both Paul and James are talking about when they call upon Abraham as a witness.

The account of Abraham's life is told chronologically in Genesis 12–25.

6.   Read Genesis 15:6. What did Abraham do? What did God do?

Paul makes it clear that our salvation is not the result of any good works we do. To prove his point, he reminds his readers that Abraham was justified (declared righteous) by God as a gift and not by works:

For if Abraham was justified by works, he has something to boast about, but not before God. For what does the Scripture say? "Abraham believed God, and it was counted to him as righteousness." (Romans 4:2–3)

So what is James talking about in the verses we are studying this week?

Was not Abraham our father justified by works when he offered up his son Isaac on the altar? You see that faith was active along with his works, and faith was completed by his works; and the Scripture was fulfilled that says, "Abraham believed God, and it was counted to him as righteousness"—and he was called a friend of God. You see that a person is justified by works and not by faith alone. (James 2:21–24)

7.   What event in Abraham's life does James point to?

     a.   What does James say happened to Abraham's faith?

     b.   What does James say happened to the Scripture?

     c.   Which meaning of "justified" do you think James is using? What clues do you see in the text that make you think so?

In verse 23, James quotes Genesis 15, just like Paul did. But James is talking about an event that happened around thirty years later—the sacrifice of Isaac. This event is found in Genesis 22. We're *told* that Abraham believed God in Genesis 15, but in Genesis 22 we *see* that Abraham believed God. His faith was proven, or demonstrated, by his actions.

Paul and James are in complete agreement: professed faith that doesn't result in good works isn't saving faith. They also agree that works without faith won't save you. We're saved by faith alone, but that faith does not remain alone. True faith results in works of obedience, the pursuit of holiness, the cultivation of Christ's likeness, and acts of mercy. Let the words of our memory verse sink from your head to your heart and then compel the work of your hands.

MEMORY VERSE

But someone will say, "You have faith and I have works." Show me your faith apart from your works, and I will show you my faith by my works.

James 2:18

DAY 4

Application: How Does the Text Transform Me?

◆

PRAY

Father, Son, and Holy Spirit, you are the God who saves! Thank you for doing everything required to save me. I ask that you use your Word to confirm the reality of my salvation. And I ask that you would give me opportunities to live out my salvation through works you have prepared for me. Amen.

READ JAMES 2:14–26

We saw in the homework on Day 2 that the relationship between salvation, faith, and works is best depicted as Faith = Salvation + Works. We're saved by faith alone, but, once we're saved, that faith doesn't remain alone. We can fall into error on both sides of this equation. We can think that our works contribute to our salvation or we can believe that a profession of faith that never results in a changed life is real faith.

Jesus came not only to save us, he came to redeem and restore us. Our salvation isn't only for the life to come; it's for the life here and now. When Jesus saves us, he intends to transform us. Our transformation is to be holistic, affecting not only our heads (what we think), but also our hearts (what we love) and our hands (what we do).

1. In what ways can you see that your salvation has transformed not just your head, but also your heart and your hands?

2. Using the example James gave in verses 15–16, when was the last time you encountered someone in need of physical provisions?

    a. How did you respond?

    b. Why did you respond this way?

3. When you give to someone in need, what is your motivation?

4. In what ways are you tempted to think of your profession of faith as separate from any good deeds?

5. In what ways do you think (or want) your good works to justify (first definition, pg. 80) you? Why?

Do you know anyone who would readily say, "I believe in God," but has no other indicator of Christian faith? To that person, James's words are quite chilling. He makes it abundantly clear that a profession of faith is in no way the same thing as a possession of faith. He offers demons as an example of those who would fully acknowledge an orthodox understanding of God and even respond to that belief with an emotional response—they shudder.

Deuteronomy 6:4–5 says, "Hear, O Israel: The LORD our God, the LORD is one. You shall love the LORD your God with all your heart and with all your soul and with all your might."

6. James has told us that the demons believe the first part of these verses—that God is one.

    a. What response are they lacking according to our Deuteronomy verses?

    b. How does verse 5 show that we are to do more than profess that God is one?

7. Abraham had real faith. As a result, he obeyed God. How has your faith caused you to obey, even when it was difficult? In what way is God calling you to obey him today?

8. Rahab had real faith. As a result, she trusted God. How has your faith caused you to trust God? In what way do you need to trust him today?

9. James has offered a strong warning to anyone who claims to have faith. How can you respond to his warning today?

If you profess faith in Christ, I hope that these verses in James have confirmed the reality of that faith, and spurred you on to good works. But, you may have realized that your profession of faith hasn't significantly changed how you interact with and love your neighbor, or that you're not inclined to do good for others when it has no self-benefit. If that's you, use this opportunity to thank God that his Word has proven to be a clear mirror and ask him to give you saving faith. When you ask, he will. And as you seek him, you will be changed! May God produce many good works in and through each of us as a result of our great salvation.

MEMORY VERSE

But someone will say, "You have faith and I have works." Show me your faith apart from your works, and I will show you my faith by my works.

James 2:18

DAY 5

Reflection

◆

After all the talk this week about whether or not we're saved by works, I want to end by saying that we actually *are* saved by works. But, before you think I'm a heretic, let me clarify. We're not saved by our works; we're saved by the work of Christ.

Jesus *did* certain things. Works. It's because he did them, and did them perfectly, that we can be saved. All three members of the Trinity play a part in our salvation. Scholars clarify that salvation is planned by the Father, accomplished by the Son[12], and applied by the Holy Spirit. Meaning, our salvation was planned in eternity past. But it began to be accomplished when the Son of God took on flesh and was born as a baby in Bethlehem. We call this the *incarnation*, and it's the first work done for the accomplishment of our salvation.

Jesus then led a *perfectly sinless life*. He obeyed his Father in every way and he submitted to his Father's plan (Matt. 26:39). He was tempted but did not sin (Heb. 4:15). Each of these works, the incarnation and the sinless life, were necessary for our salvation. And they each had to happen before the next two central events could occur.

The two central events in Jesus's life—his *death and resurrection*—are the core of his saving work. Salvation was accomplished on the cross and proven to be effective in the resurrection. At the cross, Jesus paid the penalty for our sin, and in the resurrection, he proved that the payment was accepted.

After the resurrection, Jesus returned to heaven (we call this the *ascension*), sat down on his throne (we call this his *session*), poured out his Spirit (we call this *Pentecost*), and continually prays for us (we call this his *intercession*). These are each part of his saving work. The last thing Christ will do to complete our salvation is *come again*. We long for that day, when faith will be sight!

These are the works of Christ, the things he did to save us. When he gives us the gift of faith and we believe, the Holy Spirit then applies everything Jesus did to us. His perfectly sinless life is counted as our perfectly sinless life. His death becomes our death. His resurrection is our resurrection. His access to the Father becomes our access to the Father. One day, he will come again and take us to live with him, and we will reign and rule with him in glory. He has accomplished for us what we could never do for ourselves. Hallelu-jah, what a Savior!

1. Take five minutes to summarize what you've learned this week and then use those thoughts to journal and guide your prayer.

2. Try to write the memory verse for this week's chapter, without looking at it!

GROUP DISCUSSION QUESTIONS

◆

ICEBREAKER: What is your least favorite part of housework or yardwork?

WARM-UP: What are some things you've seen others do that you would consider to be good works or deeds?

Have someone (or several people) read James 2:14–26 out loud.

1. What are some ways you have been offered (or offered others) well-meaning words but not real help?

2. How has our culture shaped our thinking about the ways we help those in need of food and clothing?

3. How do you typically respond to someone in need of food and clothing? How might your response change in light of this chapter?

4. How has this chapter challenged your thoughts about the relationship between faith and works?

5. Describe the difference between the role of works pre-salvation and the role of works post-salvation? Why is this distinction so important?

6. Are you more prone to believe that your good works contribute to your salvation or that you don't need good works to validate your salvation? How do you see this play out in your life?

7. Describe a time God gave you the opportunity to show the reality of your faith either through an act of love or an act of obedience. How did you respond?

8. How has the gospel affected your head, your heart, and your hands?

9. How does thinking about all Christ has done to accomplish your salvation help you rest in the finished work of Christ (as opposed to trying to earn your salvation)?

10. What was one thing that stood out/convicted/encouraged/instructed you this week?

CHAPTER 4

Steadfast Speech: A Mighty Little Tongue

◆

JAMES 3:1–12

(1) Not many of you should become teachers, my brothers*, for you know that we who teach will be judged with greater strictness. (2) For we all stumble in many ways. And if anyone does not stumble in what he says, he is a perfect man, able also to bridle his whole body. (3) If we put bits into the mouths of horses so that they obey us, we guide their whole bodies as well. (4) Look at the ships also: though they are so large and are driven by strong winds, they are guided by a very small rudder wherever the will of the pilot directs. (5) So also the tongue is a small member, yet it boasts of great things.

How great a forest is set ablaze by such a small fire! (6) And the tongue is a fire, a world of unrighteousness. The tongue is set among our members, staining the whole body, setting on fire the entire course of life, and set on fire by hell. (7) For every kind of beast and bird, of reptile and sea creature, can be tamed and has been tamed by mankind, (8) but no human being can tame the tongue. It is a restless evil, full of deadly poison. (9) With it we bless our Lord and Father, and with it we curse people who are made in the likeness of God. (10) From the same mouth come blessing and cursing. My brothers, these things ought not to be so. (11) Does a spring pour forth from the same opening both fresh and salt water? (12) Can a fig tree, my brothers, bear olives, or a grapevine produce figs? Neither can a salt pond yield fresh water.

* Or "brothers and sisters." The Greek word *adelphoi* is plural and can refer to both men and women who are siblings in the spiritual family of God.

DAY 1

Observation: What Does the Text Say?

◆

PRAY

Lord, please take your perfect Word and use it to shine a light into the recesses of my heart. Help me to see the reality of my speech and not make excuses, but pursue your perfect and holy will for my tongue. Transform me more into the likeness of your perfect Son. Thank you. Amen.

READ JAMES 1–5

We're midway through our study! Take time today to go back and read all five chapters of James—it's a helpful way to review what we've studied so far and to consider the book in its full context. After you've done that, *read James 3:1–12* (if possible, read it out loud).

Remember, today is the day we just observe the text and ask questions like *who, what, when, where, why,* and *how.*

1.   Go back through the provided text:

    a.   Mark any words or phrases that stand out to you. Make note of patterns, key phrases, and repeated words.

    b.   Write in the margin two to three things that stand out or questions you might have.

The human tongue is approximately 3 inches long, weighs about 2.5 ounces, and is a slab of muscle covered with a mucous membrane.

It helps us chew, taste, swallow, and speak. It's simultaneously one of the more necessary and less attractive parts of our human bodies.

James talks a lot about the human tongue in these verses and he uses the word in both a literal and metaphorical sense. Because the tongue literally helps us to speak, James uses it to metaphorically represent all of the ways we use words—those we think, those we speak, and those we write. In the previous chapter, we saw that James was deeply concerned about the works of a true Christian. He now turns his attention to the words of a true Christian and how they will be the identifying mark of maturity in the life of a believer.

2.   In the verses below, what has James already said about words—both ours and God's?

- James 1:18

- James 1:19

- James 1:21

- James 1:22–23

- James 2:12

3.   What reason does James give for his warning against wanting to become a teacher?

4.   What word does James use to describe the person who never stumbles in what they say?

a. This is the same word James used in 1:4. What did we say it meant there (pg. 12)?

b. What's the benefit for the person who can control her tongue?

5. What are the first two word pictures James uses to describe the tongue?

Both a bit and a rudder are very small in comparison to the thing they control—the horse and the ship. A bit is just a small piece of metal put into a horse's mouth and held in place by the bridle. A rudder is a small piece of equipment found on the back end of a boat that remains underwater. Both help determine the direction of the body to which they are connected.[13]

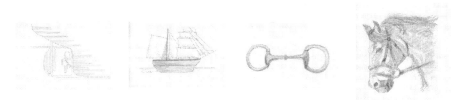

6. Using this information along with verses 3 and 4, answer the following questions:

a. What do the bit and the rudder represent?

b.   Who do the rider and the ship captain represent?

c.   What do you think the horse and the ship represent?

7.   Fill in the blanks:

a.   A ship is _____ by strong winds.

b.   A ship is _____ by a small rudder.

A bit and a rudder are neither inherently good nor bad. They're helpful if used correctly and unhelpful if used incorrectly. Their benefit depends on how they're used. The point James is making is that something so small, like the tongue, can have a huge effect on something much larger, like an entire person and the course of her life. In the same way that the rider or captain direct the horse or ship by controlling the bit or rudder, so we also are able to direct our lives toward righteous paths as we learn to control our tongues. But James now turns to his third illustration, one which lacks the possibility of a positive effect.

8.   Describe the next word picture James uses.

9. What does James say about the tongue in verse 6 (fill in the blanks)?

    a. _____ the whole body,

    b. setting on fire the entire _____ of _____,

    c. set on fire by _____.

10. What does James say has been tamed by mankind?

    a. Give an example of each (ex. sea creature: we have tamed whales and dolphins).

    b. Which one of the examples you gave do you think would be the hardest to tame? What does James say is harder still?

11. What two things does James say the tongue can be used for in verses 9 and 10?

12. What does James say about this reality?

13. What three images are given in verses 11–12?

As you study the memory verse, ask the Lord to give you insight into the words that come out of your mouth. Ask him to help you see them the way he sees them and hear them the way others hear them. Ask God to help you restrain the words that tear down and pour forth words that bring life.

MEMORY VERSE

From the same mouth come blessing and cursing.
My brothers, these things ought not to be so.

James 3:10

DAY 2

Interpretation: What Does the Text Mean?

◆

PRAY

Father, I desperately want to control my tongue. I confess that I struggle with saying things I shouldn't say and using my words to tear down rather than to build up. Please forgive me and use your Word to show me how my words can become life-giving. Amen.

READ JAMES 3:1-12

If you've ever played charades, you know it's possible to communicate without using words, but it's not easy. Words help us convey our thoughts more precisely than anything else. Words set us apart from every other creature in God's creation. But, for all the ways words help us, they also hurt us. Because we're broken, sinful people, we use our words in ways we ought not. My hope is, as we study James's words, our words will become more aligned with God's purposes.

1. James advises that not many should become teachers (in the church). Why do you think someone might want to become a teacher?

2. James tells us "we who teach will be judged with greater strictness" (verse 1).

    a. In what ways are teachers judged more strictly by others?

    b. Why do you think they might be judged more strictly by God?

3. James has already admonished us to be slow to speak (1:19). With this in mind, why is the word "stumble" a good description of ways we can sin with our words?

4.   Combine the thoughts of James 3:2 and 1:26 into one sentence.

I've been around horses my whole life. They're amazing creatures for a myriad of reasons, but I've never ceased being amazed that such a large, powerful animal is able and willing to be tamed and ridden. When a young horse is ready to begin the process, one of the first things it needs to learn is to take the bit. As the horse learns to yield to the bit, it becomes a disciplined, controlled, and useable animal. It becomes more of what it was created to be.

James is saying that our tongues are like a bit. The more controlled our tongue is, the more disciplined, controlled, and usable we are—and the more we become who we were created to be. We bear God's image accurately, speak words of blessing, and proclaim the excellencies of Jesus.

5.   What are the similarities between controlling a horse with a bit and controlling the tongue?

6.   If a ship is driven by strong winds and guided by a small rudder, how can the tongue be like a rudder in the "strong winds" of life?

We've all seen the devastating results of the wildfires that especially plague the western half of the United States. Every year, vast amounts of trees, homes, properties, and even lives are lost due to the destructive and devastating nature of fire. The fires get quickly out of control and take many days and many people to stop them.

Even after the fires are stopped, the burned places remain charred for years.

7. The destructive image of a fire helps us better understand James's concern for how we use our tongues.

    a. How can our tongues cause destruction and devastation?

    b. How can our words get quickly out of control?

    c. How can the devastation of our words be hard to remedy?

8. Make a list of as many words as you can think of that refer to how a person can use the tongue for evil (lying, sarcasm, etc.).

9. In verse 8, James calls the tongue a "restless evil, full of deadly poison." What kind of creature does it sound like James is describing? What significance could this description have?

10. Why do you think James mentions that people are made in the likeness of God?

11. What does it mean that something "ought not to be so"?

12. What would you think if you saw an apple tree with oranges on it? What does this have to do with our words?

Chances are, you're feeling the weight of James's words. I am! We've all used words in hurtful ways. And we've all had words spoken to us that hurt. Words are powerful. As you sit under the authority of God's perfect Word, let it both convict and heal.

MEMORY VERSE

From the same mouth come blessing and cursing.
My brothers, these things ought not to be so.

James 3:10

DAY 3

Interpretation: What Do Other Scriptures Say?

◆

PRAY

Father, your Word is life! I don't live by bread alone, but I live by every word that comes from you. I ask you to give me an insatiable hunger for your Word. Use your Word to feed, nourish, and strengthen me today—that my words may be filled with your Word. In Jesus's name I pray. Amen.

READ JAMES 3:1–12

Words are powerful. We use them to persuade, deter, build up, instruct, make someone laugh, and make someone cry. Our words shape us, shape others, and reveal what's truly in us. James wants his readers to recognize the power of their words and submit them to the life-changing power of God's Word.

1. Read Isaiah 6:1–5. When Isaiah was confronted with the holiness of God, why do you think his response was to cry out that he was "a man of unclean lips"?

2. Read Isaiah 50:4.

    a. What did God give Isaiah?

b.   Why?

c.   How?

d.   When?

The Bible does not say no one should teach. Isaiah was a prophet and was called to instruct and teach people. James was also a teacher. Paul said that the Lord gives teachers to the church (Eph. 4:11). We're all commanded to teach the next generation about the Lord (Ps. 78:5–6).

3.   Read Mark 12:38–40. How does this help us better understand James's warning against wanting to become a teacher?

4.   Read Matthew 15:10–11; 15–20.

> And he called the people to him and said to them, "Hear and understand: it is not what goes into the mouth that defiles a person, but what comes out of the mouth; this defiles a person." ... But Peter said to him, "Explain the parable to us." And he said, "Are you also still without understanding? Do you not see that whatever goes into the mouth passes into the stomach and is expelled? But what comes out of the mouth proceeds from the heart, and this defiles a person. For out of the heart come

evil thoughts, murder, adultery, sexual immorality, theft, false witness, slander. These are what defile a person. But to eat with unwashed hands does not defile anyone."

a.   What does Jesus say defiles a person?

b.   Where do our words originate?

5.   Read the following verses and write down the connection you see between the heart and the mouth.

Ps. 19:14 Let the words of my mouth and the meditation of my heart be accept-able in your sight, o LORD, my rock and my redeemer.	
Ps. 49:3 My mouth shall speak wisdom; the meditation of my heart shall be understanding.	
Rom 10:9 because, if you confess with your mouth that Jesus is Lord and believe in your heart that God raised him from the dead, you will be saved.	

| Rom 10:10 | |
| For with the heart one believes and is justified, and with the mouth one confesses and is saved. | |

6. Read Matthew 12:33–37.

    a. What similarities do you see between Jesus's words and the passage we're studying in James this week?

    b. Why do you think Jesus says "by your words you will be justified"?

    c. Thinking of the work you did last week (pg. 80), which definition of justified do you think Jesus is using?

    d. What has to be mastered before we can hope to master the tongue?

7. Read the following passage from John 8:44.

    Jesus told the unbelieving Jews, "You are of your father the devil, and your will is to do your father's desires. He was a murderer from the beginning, and does not stand in the truth, because there is no truth in him. When he lies, he speaks out of his own character, for he is a liar and the father of lies."

a.   What is the devil called?

b.   Why?

8.   Read Genesis 3:1. What did the serpent question?

It's important to remember that the devil still does both of these—he lies and he wants us to doubt God's Word. He twists God's Word, asks us to doubt God's Word, and his ultimate desire is for us to believe him instead of believing God. Like Eve, we choose whose word we will believe, and our words will reflect our choice.

9.   Read Proverbs 16:27–28.

a.   What word is used to describe the person? What image is used that James used, too?

b.   How does a whisperer separate close friends? How is gossip like kindling for a fire?

10. Read Proverbs 12:18. What do rash words do? What do the words of the wise do?

If you're like me, you long to have an instructed tongue like Isaiah and for your words to bring healing and life to those around you. But it's hard! The tongue really is difficult to tame. We'll spend our time tomorrow looking at how to respond to what James has said. Meanwhile, as you work on your memory verse today, ask the Lord to give you the tongue of the wise, that your words may be healing and helpful to those around you.

MEMORY VERSE

From the same mouth come blessing and cursing.
My brothers, these things ought not to be so.

James 3:10

DAY 4

Application: How Does the Text Transform Me?

◆

PRAY

Father, thank you for giving your Word to your people. Use it today to convict, rebuke, train, and instruct me. Open my eyes to see how my words could be more life-giving to those around me. Teach me to tame my tongue, restrain my speech, and pour forth words of life. Help me to use my words to praise you and bless others. In Jesus's name I pray. Amen.

READ JAMES 3:1–12

When someone's arrested, a rule called the "Miranda rights" requires the first words spoken to the accused to be, "You have the right to remain silent." This right is given in order to protect the accused from bringing further incrimination upon herself. Oh, that the Holy Spirit would whisper those words to me before I speak! Proverbs 10:19 says, "When words are many, transgression is not lacking, but whoever restrains his lips is prudent." I think if James had known of the Miranda rights, he would have said that the opening sentence is good advice, not just for the accused, but for all of us.

1. Give an example of a time when silence might be the best form of restraint, and give an example of a time when silence might not be helpful.

Remember, James wants his readers to be mature and steadfast in their faith. Part of spiritual maturity is knowing not just *what* to do, but understanding the motivation of our heart *behind* what we do. His warning to would-be-teachers is along that line: warning us that it's not just *what* we say that's important, but *why* we're saying it.

2.   Have you ever found yourself wanting others to listen to you and, consequently, think highly of you? If so, how do James's words about teachers offer a heart-check?

3.   Words have the power for good or for harm. Think back over your life—how have you experienced words that hurt? That heal? How have those words impacted you?

Ephesians 4:29–32 says, "Let no corrupting talk come out of your mouths, but only such as is good for building up, as fits the occasion, that it may give grace to those who hear. And do not grieve the Holy Spirit of God, by whom you were sealed for the day of redemption. Let all bitterness and wrath and anger and clamor and slander be put away from you, along with all malice. Be kind to one another, tenderhearted, forgiving one another, as God in Christ forgave you."

4. Using the chart below, make note of how you might have grieved the Holy Spirit by using your words in these different ways.

	VERBAL / PERSONAL INTERACTION	WRITTEN CORRESPONDENCE (EMAIL, TEXT MESSAGES, LETTERS, ETC.)	SOCIAL MEDIA POSTS
BITTERNESS			
ANGER			
WRATH			
CLAMOR			
SLANDER			
SARCASM			
LYING			
GOSSIPING			
CUSSING			
COMPLAINING / GRUMBLING			
BOASTING			

5. Which of the above attributes do you struggle with most? Why?

6. Which of the above forms of communication gets you in trouble with your words the most? Why?

7. In what ways do you try to make excuses or rationalize your communication patterns?

8. How have you experienced the destructive consequences of complaining, lying, gossip, slander, etc. in your own life?

9. Sadly, we've all said words that have been like a forest fire—destructive and out of control.

    a. Write down the names of a few people you know you've hurt with your words.

    b. If you haven't yet, take time to repent and ask God to forgive you.

    c. Prayerfully, review the names you listed. Consider whether it might be appropriate to contact any of those people and sincerely apologize—with no expectation of reciprocation.

10. James says no one has ever tamed their tongue. Does this mean we're unable to change?

    a.   We saw that the mouth speaks out of the overflow of the heart (Matt. 15:18). If we want to have words of life flowing out of our mouths, what needs to change (remember ch. 2, Day 3, question 4 – pg. 52!)?

    b.   Who is able to tame your tongue? How?

    c.   David cried out, "Create in me a clean heart, O God, and renew a right spirit within me" (Ps. 51:10). Take time now, and ask God to do the same in you.

James has already warned his readers about the double-minded man (1:8). He now warns us about the double-tongued person—the one who uses her tongue to both praise God and curse others. He argues that a tongue used to bless the Lord should not be used to curse those made in the Lord's image. This is for two reasons: 1) The same mouth should not produce both blessing and cursing; and 2) God considers our cursing of any person, because they bear his image, as a curse against himself!

11. How might the idea that God considers our cursing of another to be a curse against himself change the way you speak to (or about) others?

James uses several images to show his readers the absurdity of unwholesome talk coming out of a Christian's mouth. He says it's as ludicrous as olives growing on a fig tree or both salt and fresh water coming from the same spring. All of his illustrations highlight the fact that there should not be a discrepancy between the source and the product.

12. Fill in the following blanks and answer the following questions.

   - A spring does not produce _____ and salt water.
   - A fig tree does not produce _____, but figs.
   - A grapevine does not produce figs, but _____.
   - A salt pond does not produce _____ water.

   a. Yes or No: Do the people around you have to wonder if it's going to be (metaphorical) salt water or fresh water coming out of your mouth at any given moment?

   b. Think of the different spheres in your life: work, neighborhood, church, family circles, etc. Would one sphere be surprised if they overheard you speaking in another sphere? How so?

God's words are all-powerful (omnipotent) and life-creating because God is omnipotent and life-creating. As those created in his
image, our words, although not *omni*potent, are still potent. Our
words have power, not to be life-creating, but to be life-giving. Sadly,
because we're broken, sinful, and rebellious, our words also have
power to destroy and be life-taking. Proverbs 18:21a says, "Death
and life are in the power of the tongue."

13. Ask the Holy Spirit to help you complete the following chart:

Specific phrases and statements I use that can be life-*taking*	Specific phrases and statements I can replace these with, to be life-*giving*
Example: "What's wrong with you?"	Example: "I don't understand, but I want to."

As you work on your memory verse, ask the Lord to give you a
tongue that blesses and breathes life into others.

MEMORY VERSE

From the same mouth come blessing and cursing.
My brothers, these things ought not to be so.

James 3:10

DAY 5

Reflection

◆

Our God is a God who speaks. Speaking is the first thing we see him do in Genesis 1—and his words bring life! He spoke everything into existence: the heavens, the earth, the sun and moon, the land, the sea, the birds, and the animals. His Word brought forth life.

Once God spoke life into existence, life continued to be found in *obedience* to his Word. Adam and Eve were told to obey God's good Word. Their obedience didn't earn them all of God's good provisions; God had freely given them everything they needed. But, if they disobeyed, God said they would surely die (Gen. 2:17).

Tragically, the serpent came and tempted them to doubt God's Word. The serpent, the father of lies, spoke words of deceit and deception. When Adam and Eve believed the words of the serpent over the Word of God, death entered in and Adam and Eve were cast out of God's presence. The rejection of God's Word brought death.

As the story progresses, we see that life continues to be found in God and his Word. It's why both Moses and Jesus said, "[We] shall not live by bread alone, but by every word that comes from the mouth of the Lord" (Deut. 8:3; Matt. 4:4). Moses, at the end of his life and ministry, pleaded with Israel saying, "For it is no empty word for you, but your very life, and by this word you shall live…" (Deut. 32:47). Likewise, the psalmist, centuries later, cried out, "My soul clings to the dust; give me life according to your word!"(Ps. 119:25). God's Word is life.

Ultimately, we're brought from death to life by the incarnate Word of God—Jesus—who took on flesh and dwelt among us. John tells us:

> In the beginning was the Word, and the Word was with God, and the Word was God. He was in the beginning with God. All things were made through him, and without him was not any thing made that was made. In him was life, and the life was the light of men. (John 1:1–4)

Jesus told his disciples, "Whoever hears my word and believes him who sent me has eternal life. He does not come into judgment, but has passed from death to life" (John 5:24). James has already told us that we have been "brought forth by the word of truth" (James 1:18). God's Word saves us and gives us eternal life.

We're people created by the Word of God, saved by the Word of God, nourished and strengthened by the Word of God. His Word is powerful and mighty to save. As a result, our words matter. We'll be held account for every word we utter, both privately and publicly. This reality may want to make us buy a big role of duct tape to use on our mouths as a preventative measure. However, our words simply expose the reality of what's happening in our hearts. God changes us from the inside out. May we be women who are instructed by and conformed to the Word of God. And may our words be evidence of the fact that we have been saved by the Word himself.

1. Take five minutes to summarize what you've learned this week and then use those thoughts to journal and guide your prayer.

2. Try to write the memory verse for this week's chapter, without looking at it!

GROUP DISCUSSION QUESTIONS

◆

ICEBREAKER: What is one of your most or least favorite words?

WARM-UP: Share with your group one of the kindest things said to you recently.

Have someone (or several people) read James 3:1–12 out loud.

1. Why do you think we tend to judge teachers in the church more strictly? Do you think this is right?

2. What are some practical ways you have attempted to bridle your tongue?

3. What are some examples of life-giving speech? Which of these is most difficult for you and why?

4. What are some examples of life-taking speech? Which of these do you struggle with most and why?

5. What kind of words are life-giving for you to hear (or read)? What kind of words are the most poisonous?

6. Describe how someone else's words can be like the spark that sets our own tongue on fire. How can we use our words to stop this destructive pattern?

7. Describe a time when your tongue felt restless and hard to control. How might this passage help you with a similar struggle in the future?

8. How can we encourage each other to have tamed and instructed tongues? What would this look like practically when we're with a group of women and we hear gossip or complaining? Bitterness or sarcasm? How can we lovingly steer the conversation toward life-giving words?

9. How does the Word of God shape our words?

10. What was one thing that stood out/convicted/encouraged/instructed you this week?

Steadfast Wisdom: A Harvest of Righteousness

◆

JAMES 3:13–4:12

(13) Who is wise and understanding among you? By his good conduct let him show his works in the meekness of wisdom. (14) But if you have bitter jealousy and selfish ambition in your hearts, do not boast and be false to the truth. (15) This is not the wisdom that comes down from above, but is earthly, unspiritual, demonic. (16) For where jealousy and selfish ambition exist, there will be disorder and every vile practice. (17) But the wisdom from above is first pure, then peaceable, gentle, open to reason, full of mercy and good fruits, impartial and sincere. (18) And a harvest of righteousness is sown in peace by those who make peace.

(1) What causes quarrels and what causes fights among you? Is it not this, that your passions are at war within you? (2)

You desire and do not have, so you murder. You covet and cannot obtain, so you fight and quarrel. You do not have, because you do not ask. (3) You ask and do not receive, because you ask wrongly, to spend it on your passions. (4) You adulterous people! Do you not know that friendship with the world is enmity with God? Therefore whoever wishes to be a friend of the world makes himself an enemy of God. (5) Or do you suppose it is to no purpose that the Scripture says, "He yearns jealously over the spirit that he has made to dwell in us"? (6) But he gives more grace. Therefore it says, "God opposes the proud but gives grace to the humble." (7) Submit yourselves therefore to God. Resist the devil, and he will flee from you. (8) Draw near to God, and he will draw near to you. Cleanse your hands, you sinners, and purify your hearts, you double-minded. (9) Be wretched and mourn and weep. Let your laughter be turned to mourning and your joy to gloom. (10) Humble yourselves before the Lord, and he will exalt you.

(11) Do not speak evil against one another, brothers*. The one who speaks against a brother or judges his brother, speaks evil against the law and judges the law. But if

you judge the law, you are not a doer of the law but a judge. (12) There is only one lawgiver and judge, he who is able to save and to destroy. But who are you to judge your neighbor?

* Or "brothers and sisters." The Greek word *adelphoi* is plural and can refer to both men and women who are siblings in the spiritual family of God.

DAY 1

Observation: What Does the Text Say?

◆

PRAY

Father, Son, and Holy Spirit, thank you for the gift of your Word. You're the source of all wisdom and I ask that you grant me, Holy Spirit, insight and understanding as I study. Use my time in your Word to conform me to the image of Christ. Humble me and teach me according to your great grace. In Christ's name I pray. Amen.

READ JAMES 3:13–4:12 (IF POSSIBLE, READ IT OUT LOUD.)

Remember, today is the day we just observe the text and ask questions like *who, what, when, where, why,* and *how*.

1. Go back through the provided text:

    a. Mark any words or phrases that stand out to you. Make note of patterns, key phrases, and repeated words.

    b. Write in the margin two to three things that stand out or questions you might have.

In the last few chapters, James's focus has been on works and words, but he now returns to a topic he introduced in chapter 1—wisdom. In the same way he contrasted true and false faith in chapter 2, James now wants his readers to understand the difference between true and false wisdom. True wisdom, he says, will be demonstrated through both what we do and what we say because wisdom is to rule both our words and our works.

2.   How will the wise person show she is wise?

3.   What two things does James identify in both verse 14 and 16 as root issues of discord?

4.   Read James 3:15–18 and fill in the chart.[14]

	False Wisdom (verses 15–16)	True Wisdom (verses 17–18)
Origin		
Characteristics		
Results		

5.   Looking back: We've seen the phrase "from above" before in James 1:17.

   a.   In James 1:17, what does he tell us comes from above?

   b.   According to James 1:5, what gift does God give? How does he give it?

James wraps up his conversation about wisdom by saying that those who possess wisdom from above will be peaceable. They will sow seeds of righteousness in peace, and they will be people who make peace. The wise person is clearly a person who brings peace to a situation. But as we move into chapter 4, there's a stark contrast. The next verse contains the words *quarrels, fights,* and *war.*

6. What are the three answers James gives to the rhetorical question he poses in 4:1?

7. What two reasons does James give to his statement, "You do not have"?

8. Fill in these two blanks according to verse 2:

    a. You desire but don't get _____.

    b. You _____ but cannot obtain so you fight and quarrel.

9. Read verse 6b and fill in the chart below:

Posture of the Person	What God Does

Posture of the Person	What God Does

10. In verses 7–10, James gives nine imperatives (or commands). List them, using the first letter prompts provided for each one.

- S
- R
- D
- C
- P
- Be W
- M
- W
- H

a. What do the first and the last have in common?

b. Write each phrase below next to the command that precedes it in the list above:

    i.   he will flee from you
    ii. he will draw near to you
    iii. he will exalt you

c. Write down the two scenarios in verses 7 and 10 stating what God does, what we're to do, and what the devil will do.

    i.   When   I _____,   God   will

    _____.

    ii.   When I _____, the devil will

    _____.

11. There are several repeated words in verses 11–12. Which word is repeated most?

12. The NIV renders verse 11b, "When you judge the law, you are not keeping it, but sitting in judgment on it." What two options does James give for how we can interact with the law?

We can _____ the law.

Or we can _____ the law.

The wise person will strive for peace whenever possible and do battle, not with others, but with the desires in her own heart. She won't be jealous or have selfish ambition. And she certainly won't speak evil against her brothers and sisters. She will be humble and entrust herself to the Lord, the righteous Judge. As you study your memory verse for this week, ask the Lord to give you the wisdom that is from above, grant you humility, and give you more of his grace.

MEMORY VERSE

But he gives more grace. Therefore it says, "God opposes the proud, but gives grace to the humble."

James 4:6

DAY 2

Interpretation: What Does the Text Mean?

◆

PRAY

Father, as I come to your Word today, I confess that I don't always walk in wisdom. I can be quarrelsome and jealous. Teach me, Lord, to humble myself before you and those around me. And please, draw near to me as I draw near to you through your Word. In Jesus's mighty name, Amen.

READ JAMES 3:13–4:12

1. Name some qualities a person would need to possess for you to identify them as wise.

Often, we can think that wisdom has to do with IQ, education, degrees, or knowledge. But we can have those without possessing any real wisdom. We all probably know someone who's "educated," but lacks a beautiful lifestyle. Conversely, we probably all know someone lacking formal education, but full of wisdom from above—someone whose life is marked by the beauty of wisdom: peaceable relationships, good deeds, kind words, and increasing holiness.

In addition to the idea that wisdom is visible in good conduct or a beautiful lifestyle, James also says that it can be seen in meekness.

2.   What words come to mind when you hear the word "meekness"?

A lot of people think that *meekness* is synonymous with *weakness*. In fact, if you look it up in a dictionary, most of the definitions have a negative connotation, saying things like, *overly submissive, spiritless,* and *resignation*. But that's not the way James—or Jesus—uses the word. Meekness is actually strength reigned in, under control, and willingly submissive. It's not the absence of strength, but the proper restraint of it. Paul even refers to the "meekness of Christ" (2 Cor. 10:1). We know that Jesus was not weak! But he certainly allowed his strength to be reigned in, willingly submitting himself to his Father's will.

3.   How does meekness relate to godly wisdom?

4.   In what ways are humility and submitting to God related?

When James asks, "What causes quarrels and what causes fights among you?"(4:1), we have to remember that he's writing to believers, to the church. Sadly, quarrels and fights within churches and between Christians are not uncommon.

5.   What are some desires that can cause conflict in the church or among believers?

James says that we each have passions that wage war within us. These passions are things we want and, when we don't get them, we fight with those we think are preventing us from having the thing or things we desire. The Greek word for "passions" is *hēdonē,* which is where we get our English word *hedonism.* James uses this same word again at the end of verse 3 where some translations use the word *pleasures.*

6.   Look up the word *hedonism* in a dictionary and write down the definition.

      a.   What insight do you gain when realizing that verse 3 could read, "You ask and do not receive, because you ask wrongly, to spend it on your 'own hedonistic pleasures"?

      b.   How do both words (passions and pleasures) help us understand what James is saying?

7. Instead of fighting for what we want, what are we supposed to do, according to verse 2?

Hedonism, at its root, is a love of the things this world can offer. We pay billions of dollars each year in order to amuse ourselves through entertainment, shopping, eating, professional athletics, vacations, and travel. None of these things are inherently bad. They become bad when our desire for them outweighs our desire for God—when we seek our own pleasure more than we seek God himself. This is what led James to use the word "adulterous" as an adjective for anyone who loves the pleasures of this world more than they love God.

8. In what way is "adulterous" an accurate description of someone who's in "friendship (or love) with the world"?

9. What do you think the word "therefore" in verse 7 refers to?

There's always a connection between God's grace and our obedience. One commentator said it like this, "The God who says 'Here is my grace to receive' says in the same breath, 'Here are my commands to obey.'"[15] His grace always precedes our obedience! This is important to remember for two reasons—first, our obedience doesn't earn God's grace or love, and secondly, our obedience is proof that we have received his grace. We are unable to obey on our own. But praise be to God, he gives us more grace!

10. Next to each of the commands from verses 7–10, comment on how obeying the command might serve to diminish quarreling and fighting.

- ·   Submit yourself to God:
- ·   Resist the devil:
- ·   Draw near to God:
- ·   Cleanse your hands:
- ·   Purify your heart:
- ·   Be wretched, mourn and weep (over your sin):
- ·   Humble yourself before the Lord:

11. What law has James already mentioned (hint: James 2:8) that is most likely in view here?

   a.   How do you think "speaking against" and "judging" are related to each other?

   b.   How is judging the opposite of loving?

The word *humble* is used only twice in the section we're studying this week, yet humility is the principle that holds these verses together. It takes humility to be meek. It takes humility to walk in the wisdom from above instead of in earthly wisdom—trusting in God's ways and not our own. It takes humility to lay down selfish desires and desire the good of others. It takes humility to ask for more grace, submit yourself to God, and weep over sin. It takes humility to realize that you don't have the ability or right to judge the motives of others, but to entrust that person to the only good and righteous Judge.

So, James tells us to humble ourselves. When we do, we will find that God gives even more grace! As you meditate on your memory verse for this week, ask the Lord to give you the grace needed to trust him and humble yourself before him and before others.

MEMORY VERSE

But he gives more grace. Therefore it says, "God opposes the proud, but gives grace to the humble."

James 4:6

DAY 3

Interpretation: What Do Other Scriptures Say?

◆

PRAY

Father, you're the giver of all good and perfect gifts. Thank you most of all for the gift of your perfect Son. Thank you that, in him, we find grace upon grace. I ask that your grace would enable me today to walk in obedience to your commands. Give me an opportunity to humble myself, trust you, and experience the joy of both. In Jesus's name I pray. Amen.

READ JAMES 3:13-4:12

Scripture presents Godly wisdom as a good thing to desire. The book of Proverbs begins with an exaltation of wisdom and a plea from a father to his son to pursue wisdom as the greatest virtue. Wisdom is personified as a beautiful, noble woman who will protect, help, and bless the person who pursues her. Ultimately, we know that it's in "Christ in whom are hidden all the treasures of wisdom and knowledge" (Col. 2:3). As we pursue Christ, we're pursuing his wisdom, which he gives generously to his people (James 1:5).

1. Read Job 28:28.

    a. According to this verse, what is wisdom and what is understanding?

    b. Rewrite James 3:13 using your answers above to replace "wise" and "understanding."

It's a bit heartbreaking and sobering to remember that James is writing to the church. When he calls out selfishness, jealousy, covetousness, pride, slander, condemnation, selfish ambition, and envy, he's identifying things he sees in fellow believers in the same congregations—the quarrels and fights are among members of the same church. Friends, this should not be!

2. Read Galatians 5:18–23. Using the chart below, list all of the acts of the flesh and fruit of the Spirit Paul mentions. After you've

made your lists, underline every word in each column that
James also addresses.

ACTS OF THE FLESH	FRUIT OF THE SPIRIT

3.   Read Philippians 2:3. What's the antidote to our selfish ambition?

4.   Read Luke 8:14 (The word for "pleasures" is the same word
     James uses for passions).

   a.   Not only does our passion for pleasure cause us to war with
        others, according to Jesus, what else does it do?

   b.   What does not mature as a result?

   c.   How does this relate to question 2 above?

As we saw yesterday, our hedonistic desires are at the root of our
conflicts, quarrels, and fights. If we're ruled by our passions and our

desire for the pleasures of this world, we'll not only fight and quarrel with others, we'll be stunted in our Christian growth; the fruit of the Spirit will not be produced in us, and we won't mature in our faith. Hedonism is a thorn that chokes out spiritual maturity, the fruit of peace, and a harvest of righteousness.

5. Read Matthew 7:7–11. James told us that we do not have because we do not ask. What confidence and comfort do these verses offer you in prayer?

James also said that we don't get what we ask for in prayer because we ask wrongly. We ask for things in order to satisfy our desire for our own pleasure.

6. Read 1 John 5:14. What's the caveat to getting anything we ask for?

God is not opposed to our desires for pleasure and satisfaction. In fact, he created us to experience delight, joy, and pleasure. The problem is that our desires can be misguided and we can seek for satisfaction and joy in things that were never meant to provide it.

7. Read Psalm 16:11.

    a. Where is fullness of joy found?

    b. What is at God's right hand?

John Piper coined the phrase "Christian hedonism." He explains that if we truly understood ourselves, we would realize that our greatest pleasures, deepest desires, and ultimate delights are found in God himself. Piper argues that a person's desire to be happy is perfectly aligned with God's desire for his own glory because "God is most glorified in me when I am most satisfied in him."[16] God's not opposed to our desires for pleasure and satisfaction. He just knows that our ultimate delight is found in him.

8.   Read Psalm 37:4. How are the desires mentioned here different than the desires James is talking about?

9.   In what ways do the following verses help you understand James 4:4–5?

      ·   Isaiah 54:5: For your Maker is your husband, the LORD of hosts is his name; and the Holy One of Israel is your Redeemer, the God of the whole earth he is called.

      ·   1 Corinthians 6:19–20a: Or do you not know that your body is a temple of the Holy Spirit within you, whom you have from God? You are not your own, for you were bought with a price.

      ·   Matthew 6:24: No one can serve two masters, for either he will hate the one and love the other, or he will be devoted to the one and despise the other. You cannot serve God and money.

10. Read Matthew 4:1–11. How did Jesus live out James 4:7?

11. Read Matthew 7:1–6. What two reasons are given for why we shouldn't judge others?

12. Isaiah 33:22 tells us: "For the LORD is our judge; the LORD is our lawgiver; the LORD is our king; he will save us."

    a.   According to Isaiah 33:22, fill in the blanks: The Lord is our _____, our _____, and our _____.

    b.   What will he do?

    c.   What insight does this verse offer us in our understanding of James 4:12?

Our passage this week has reminded us that God is our wisdom, so we're to seek him. He's our delight, so we're to love him. And, he's our judge, so we're to submit to him. I love that Isaiah ends verse 22 by reminding us that he's also our Savior—which means that we're to worship him!

As a result, draw near to God as you work on your memory verse for this week. He loves you, delights in you, and saves you . . . and he will draw near to you.

MEMORY VERSE

But he gives more grace. Therefore it says, "God opposes the proud, but gives grace to the humble."

James 4:6

DAY 4

Application: How Does the Text Transform Me?

◆

PRAY

Father, I know your Word is meant to do more than just inform me—it's meant to transform me into the image of your Son. Holy Spirit, please use my time in your Word to correct, instruct, nourish, rebuke, and encourage me. I ask that the wisdom from above would produce a harvest of righteousness in me. In Jesus's name I pray. Amen.

READ JAMES 3:13–4:12

James wrote his epistle in the First century. But today, in the twenty-first century, our need to know how to answer James's question in 3:13 ("who is wise and understanding among you?") is as crucial now as it was then—maybe even more so. We have access to so many voices, so many opinions, and so much teaching that it can be overwhelming and confusing. It can be difficult to discern who is truly wise. James helps us understand the difficulty.

The first mark of true wisdom is the evidence of a beautiful lifestyle. A truly wise person will be gentle, reasonable, full of mercy and good deeds. But so many of the people we run to for "wisdom" are not people we know personally; meaning, we're unable to verify if their lifestyle confirms their perceived wisdom.

Additionally, so many of the people we "follow," "like," or "subscribe to" would not meet James's requirements of being meek, humble, or peaceable. It doesn't take much time on social media to realize that many of our modern-day gurus exhibit jealousy, selfishness, pride, slander, and quarreling—all of the things James aligns with false wisdom.

1. How can this passage help you discern who you will consider as truly wise?

But it's not just recognizing wisdom in others. We want to possess it ourselves!

2. Fill in the blank with your name and read it out loud:

But _____ is first pure, then peaceable, gentle, open to reason, full of mercy and good fruits, impartial and sincere. (James 3:17)

    a.   Which attributes do you think fit?

    b.   Which ones don't?

    c.   Go back and read James 1:5.

I remember hearing a pastor offer a word of advice to anyone contemplating marriage. He said, "Look at the history your potential spouse has with roommates." His reasoning was, if this person had a history of changing roommates due to conflict, arguments, and fights, then, in his words, "run."

I don't think there is any reason to limit that litmus test to roommates, though. Some people are characterized by constant quarrels, disrupted and fractured relationships, and relational chaos. Siblings don't speak. Parents cut off adult children. In-laws bicker and squabble. Friendships explode. Neighbors feud. Employees quit job after job.

3.   Think through the different relationships you have (family, friends, neighbors, co-workers, and church family) and make a list of everyone you're currently in a quarrel or fight with.

I once heard a story about a woman who'd been divorced six times. As she was contemplating her track record, the thought occurred to her, "Maybe the problem isn't them. Maybe the problem is me?"

I'm not saying that you're single-handedly responsible for every conflict you named above. In fact, you may be striving for wisdom and peace in many of them, but peace is not possible for a variety of reasons. However, as God shines the light of his Word into the recesses of our hearts, we have to be willing to let him show us where our sin resides.

4.   Briefly describe the last argument you had.

     a.   Can you identify what your desire was (e.g. respect, honor, gratitude, love, power, authority . . .) that you did not get?

     b.   How would humility have changed your response?

     c.   Using some of the words from 3:17, how could you respond differently in the future?

If the above was utterly discouraging to you, take heart! James doesn't leave us there. He reminds us that God "gives more grace." Isn't that what we need? James tells us that this "more grace" is given, not to the proud, but to the humble. And then he tells us how to humble ourselves.

5. Next to each command, write one way you can obey that command today.

    ·   Submit yourself to God:

    ·   Resist the devil:

    ·   Draw near to God:

    ·   Cleanse your hands:

    ·   Purify your heart:

    ·   Be wretched, mourn and weep (over your sin):

    ·   Humble yourself before the Lord:

We're back to humility. I once heard humility described as having "a high view of God, a sane view of myself, and a generous view of others." Rick Warren has famously described humility as "not thinking less of yourself, but thinking of yourself less."[17] Both definitions are helpful—having a realistic view of myself, not over-valuing, over-exalting, or over-thinking about myself.

6. Which would help you most, having a more "sane" (i.e. reasonable, healthy, sensible) view of yourself or thinking of yourself less? Why?

One thing that gives us a more accurate view of ourselves is having an accurate view of our sin. For most of us, it's far too easy to minimize, dismiss, or even laugh at our own sin. It doesn't grieve us the

way it should. Humbling ourselves helps us see our sin more accurately, and seeing our sin more accurately humbles us.

7.   Is there a sin you need to stop minimizing, dismissing, or even
     laughing at and instead, spend time mourning and weeping
     over it in repentance?

Pride prevents us from grieving our own sin; pride also prompts us
to sit in judgement over the sins of others. In the last section of our
passage this week, James moves from talking about general quarrels and fights, to a specific relational sin—slander, or speaking evil
against someone.

8.   Which of the words below (that James has already mentioned)
     might be a motive for slander?

     Jealousy   Ambition   Boasting

     Coveting   Envy   Pride

On Day 1, you saw that the word "judge" is used six times (James
4:11–12). However, when James tells his readers not to judge, he's
not saying that believers aren't to be discerning.
     We're absolutely called to think critically and differentiate be-
tween true and false teaching, true and false faith, and good and
bad fruit. Paul commends the Bereans for working to discern true
and false teaching (Acts 17:11). Jesus told his followers that everyone
is known by the fruit they bear and that we can see good fruit and
bad fruit (Luke 6:43–45). The author of Proverbs reminds us that
it's a faithful friend who offers words of rebuke (Prov. 27:6). Church

discipline is required for an unrepentant sinner (1 Cor. 5:9–13). We need to exercise discernment in regard to truth and sin.

What James is talking about is the judgment of someone's character or motive . . . and then to slander that person as a result of our "judgement." Oh, how we need to hear these words of James today! The quick assumption of motives, the character assassination, and the division caused by judgement is rampant—even in the church.

We may act as if we're contending for the faith when, in reality, we're being quarrelsome and speaking evil against a brother or sister. A recent post on Twitter helpfully described the difference. "The goal of a quarrel," it said, is to "win the argument and exalt self." The "goal of contending" with someone over truth and sin is to "win people" and "exalt Christ."[18] May we know the difference.

9.   Describe the last time you assumed you knew someone's motives for their actions. This could be a person in your home, church, or even on social media.

   a.   What slanderous thoughts did you have, and did you share those with anyone?

   b.   Given the passage we're studying, what help does God's Word offer you?

James says that we're not only prone to judge others, but also the law. Judging the law is the opposite of submitting to it. When we submit to God's ways, we obey, trust, and follow even when we don't understand or desire to do so. But when we judge the law, we elevate ourselves above it, deciding when and what we'll obey. It's the epitome of arrogance.

10. Using what we've studied this week, answer James's three rhetorical questions in your own words.

    a.   Who is wise and understanding among you?

    b.   What causes quarrels and what causes fights among you?

    c.   Who are you to judge your neighbor?

God takes our slander seriously, he takes our arrogance seriously, and he takes our quarreling seriously. If the Lord has used his Word to convict or even rebuke you today, thank him for it. His purpose is not to wound, but to heal. Run to him, draw near to him, and trust that his grace is sufficient for you as he transforms you more into the image of his perfect Son.

MEMORY VERSE

But he gives more grace. Therefore it says, "God opposes the proud, but gives grace to the humble."

James 4:6

DAY 5

Reflection

◆

Have you seen the bumper sticker that reads "No Jesus, no peace. Know Jesus, know peace"? I'm not a big fan of bumper stickers, but this one rings true. We all long for peace, and true peace is only found in Christ. It's why Jesus is called our Prince of Peace (Isa. 9:6). He's the one who will, one day, usher in the eternal kingdom of peace. We long for that day to come. But, as is true with so many aspects of the kingdom of God, there's an aspect of what theologians call the *already-and-not-yet*: the full kingdom has not yet come, but we already experience aspects of his peace now.

There are three main types of peace available to the believer today. The first is *peace with God*. Paul said, "Therefore, since we have been justified by faith, we have peace with God through our Lord Jesus Christ" (Rom. 5:1). This is good news! Because we're born as enemies of God (Rom. 5:10), our salvation is the declaration that God has ended the war and actually adopted his enemies and made them his children. Peace with God is one of the first and most glorious results of our salvation.

The second kind of peace is the kind we all want—the *peace of God*. This is peace for the moments of our days. We're told in Philippians that there's a peace available to us that can overrule our anxiety and protect our hearts and minds (Phil. 4:6–7). We probably all know people who've walked through various trials, yet have possessed an unexplainable, even other-worldly, peace in the midst of their tribulation. Isaiah, talking about this peace, said, "You keep him in perfect peace whose mind is stayed on you, because he trusts in you" (Isa. 26:3) and the psalmist wrote, "In peace I will both lie down and sleep; for you alone, o Lord, make me dwell in safety" (Ps. 4:8).

Some of Jesus's last words to his disciples were, "Peace I leave with you; my peace I give to you. Not as the world gives do I give to you. Let not your hearts be troubled, neither let them be afraid" (John 14:27). The peace of God is a gift of kindness available to believers, and it alters the moments in our lives when fear, anxiety, and pain threaten to undo us. The peace of God enables us to remain steadfast as we fix our mind on Christ.

The last type of peace is one that's not given, but commanded—*peace with others*. In our passage this week, James rebukes his readers for their jealousy, selfishness, boasting, envy, murder, slander, condemnation, quarreling, and fighting—the antonyms and enemies of peace. In Psalm 34:14 we're told, "Turn away from evil and do good; seek peace and pursue it."

Peace with others is not something that magically happens. Just the opposite! We have to seek it, pursue it. Paul told the Corinthians, "Aim for restoration, comfort one another, agree with one another, live in peace; and the God of love and peace will be with you" (2 Cor. 13:11). It takes humility and effort. But the God of peace, the one who has reconciled you to himself by making peace with you, the one who has freely given you his peace, commands us to live at peace with each other.

Peace with God—our very lives depend on it. The peace of God—our souls long for it. Peace with others—may you and I earnestly and wholeheartedly pursue it as a glorious demonstration that we belong to the Prince of Peace.

1.   Take five minutes to summarize what you've learned this week and then use those thoughts to journal and guide your prayer.

2.   Try to write the memory verse for this week's chapter, without looking at it!

GROUP DISCUSSION
QUESTIONS

◆

ICEBREAKER: When was the last time you thought, "All I want is a little peace!"?

WARM-UP: Who is the wisest person you know?

Have someone (or several people) read James 3:13–4:12 out loud.

1. What are some examples of "earthly wisdom," and what makes them so appealing?

2. In what ways do jealousy and selfish ambition prevent us from loving our neighbor as ourselves? If you are willing, share about a time when either "bitter jealousy" or "selfish ambition" led to a disruption in a relationship.

3. How have you experienced godly wisdom to be "peaceable, gentle, open to reason, full of mercy and good fruits, impartial [or] sincere"?

4. Share with your group one desire you have that repeatedly leads to quarrels (we all have them!).

5. Do you tend to fall more on the side of not asking for things in prayer, or asking, but with wrong motives?

6. What has been the most helpful in developing your prayer life?

7. What are some things you've done to intentionally humble yourself before God or others?

8. Are you generally aware of the need to resist the devil? What are some ways we can resist him?

9. In what areas are you most tempted to judge others (e.g. their opinions, politics, lifestyle, skills and abilities, income level...)?

10. What was one thing that stood out/convicted/encouraged/instructed you this week?

Steadfast Hope: The Coming of the Lord!

•

JAMES 4:13–5:12

(13) Come now, you who say, "Today or tomorrow we will go into such and such a town and spend a year there and trade and make a profit"— (14) yet you do not know what tomorrow will bring. What is your life? For you are a mist that appears for a little time and then vanishes. (15) Instead you ought to say, "If the Lord wills, we will live and do this or that." (16) As it is, you boast in your arrogance. All such boasting is evil. (17) So whoever knows the right thing to do and fails to do it, for him it is sin.

(1) Come now, you rich, weep and howl for the miseries that are coming upon you. (2) Your riches have rotted and your garments are moth-eaten. (3) Your gold and silver have corroded, and their corrosion will be evidence against you and will eat your flesh like fire. You have laid up trea-

sure in the last days. (4) Behold, the wages of the laborers who mowed your fields, which you kept back by fraud, are crying out against you, and the cries of the harvesters have reached the ears of the Lord of hosts. (5) You have lived on the earth in luxury and in self-indulgence. You have fattened your hearts in a day of slaughter. (6) You have condemned and murdered the righteous person. He does not resist you.

(7) Be patient, therefore, brothers*, until the coming of the Lord. See how the farmer waits for the precious fruit of the earth, being patient about it, until it receives the early and the late rains. (8) You also, be patient. Establish your hearts, for the coming of the Lord is at hand. (9) Do not grumble against one another, brothers, so that you may not be judged; behold, the Judge is standing at the door. (10) As an example of suffering and patience, brothers, take the prophets who spoke in the name of the Lord. (11) Behold, we consider those blessed who remained steadfast. You have heard of the steadfastness of Job, and you have seen the purpose of the Lord, how the Lord is compassionate and merciful.

(12) But above all, my brothers, do not swear, either by heaven or by earth or by any other oath, but let your "yes" be yes and your "no" be no, so that you may not fall under condemnation.

* Or "brothers and sisters." The Greek word *adelphoi* is plural and can refer to both men and women who are siblings in the spiritual family of God.

DAY 1

Observation: What Does the Text Say?

◆

PRAY

Father, Son, and Holy Spirit, as I come to your Word this week, I ask that you would open my eyes to see what you have for me. Open my ears to hear you speak, and my heart to love what you love. I pray that you would give me the humility to receive all that you have for me in your Word. In Jesus's name I pray. Amen.

READ JAMES 4:13–5:12 (IF POSSIBLE, READ IT OUT LOUD.)

Remember, today is the day we just observe the text and ask questions like *who, what, when, where, why,* and *how*.

1. Go back through the text:

    a. Mark any words or phrases that stand out to you. Make note of patterns, key phrases, and repeated words.

    b. Write in the margin two to three things that stand out or questions you might have.

If my five-year-old had ever woken up and declared, "I'm going to the park today, the swimming pool tomorrow, and the movie theater on Saturday," I would have laughed to myself and thought, *She imagines far greater control of her life than she actually has!* Now, if she had said, "Mom, if you'll take me, I'd love to go to the park today," I probably would have said, "Sounds great!" You see, her plans were completely dependent on mine. In a much greater way, that's what James is telling us about our plans and the Lord. It's presumptuous of us to imagine more control than we actually have.

2. List the declarations of the person in verse 13 using the following categories:

WHEN	
WHERE	
WHAT	
WHY	

a. What does James call those declarations in verse 16?

b. According to verse 15, what two things are dependent on the Lord's will?

c. What are we to say instead, about our plans?

d. Based on the person in verse 13, in which of the following might she be placing her hope? (Circle all that apply.)

Her plans   Her Control   Her Profit

3. Using James's words in verse 17, how does he define sin? How does this differ from the way we normally think about sin?

The next several verses (5:1–5) are the toughest in James's entire letter. There's some question as to whether James is still addressing the believers in the churches he's writing or if he's now addressing unbelievers in their communities who have been exploiting and oppressing the poor. Because James does not mention repentance or forgiveness, but howling and misery, most commentators tend to think that the "rich" he's speaking about are unbelievers. Whether he's speaking *about* unbelievers or not, we have to remember, he's writing *to* believers. The lesson is for us: This is not how anyone should treat money or people.

4. According to verse 2, what has happened to the riches and the garments?

5. Reread James 5:3.

    a. What has happened to their gold and silver?

    b. What does the corrosion provide?

    c. What have they done with their treasure?

6. Consider the imagery in verse 4.

   a. What did the laborers do?

   b. Who has heard them?

   c. What name does James use for God in verse 4?

The ESV uses the phrase, *Lord of hosts*; the NIV says the *Lord Almighty*; the NKJV translates it as the *Lord Sabaoth*; and the NLT says the *Lord of Heaven's Armies*. It's used only one other time in the New Testament—Romans 9:29, when Paul quotes from the book of Isaiah. However, the phrase is used extensively in the Old Testament to describe God in his role as the commander of vast armies. Our God is a mighty warrior who leads legions of soldiers in the defense of his people; a general who will wage war to defend the defenseless. By using this name for God, James is reminding his readers that God is just and the One who will protect his people.

7. Why would the name "Lord of hosts" be appropriate and encouraging in the context of this verse?

8. Describe the rich person's lifestyle according to verse 5. How might this tie into what we learned last week on Day 2 (pg. 133) regarding hedonistic pleasures?

9.   What does James tell the brothers and sisters to do in chapter 5, verse 7?

     a.   What image does he use to illustrate his point?

     b.   How are they to do that according to verse 8?

10. What does James have to tell his readers to stop doing in verse 9?

11. Using the chart below, compare 5:9 and 4:11–12 from last week. Write down any similarities you see.

JAMES 4:11–12	JAMES 5:9
(11) Do not speak evil against one another, brothers. The one who speaks against a brother or judges his brother, speaks evil against the law and judges the law. But if you judge the law, you are not a doer of the law but a judge. (12) There is only one lawgiver and judge, he who is able to save and to destroy. But who are you to judge your neighbor?	(9) Do not grumble against one another, brothers, so that you may not be judged; behold, the Judge is standing at the door.

12. According to 5:11, who should be considered blessed?

   a.   Remind yourself what trials produce (1:3).

   b.   Write down the last six words of verse 11.

13. According to verse 12, what are we supposed to do and what are we not supposed to do?

Some have taken this verse to mean that Christians aren't supposed to take an oath in a court of law. But that's not the situation James is addressing. There are so many other ways we swear and make oaths. We say things like, "With God as my witness," or "I swear on the head of my firstborn child," or even "Cross my heart, hope to die, stick a thousand needles in my eye." We add these words in an attempt to convince our hearer about the truthfulness of what we've just said. The irony is, if our first words weren't believable, what makes the extra words of an "oath" believable? James wants us to be so seamlessly honest, that we don't need to add an oath of any kind. Our "yes" will mean yes and our "no" will mean no.

As you begin to work on your memory verse for this week, ask the Lord to show you places you've wrongly set your hope. James has shown us that we can hope in ourselves, our plans, our control, our profit, our riches, our lifestyles—but all of these will fail us. The only sure place to anchor our hope is in the Lord. His will is perfect, his purposes will stand, and our merciful and compassionate God is coming again. May we rest our hope in him.

MEMORY VERSE

Behold, we consider those blessed who remained steadfast. You have heard of the steadfastness of Job, and you have seen the purpose of the Lord, how the Lord is compassionate and merciful.

James 5:11

DAY 2

Interpretation: What Does the Text Mean?

◆

PRAY

Father, I long to be steadfast in all things. Use your Word today to strengthen and establish my heart, my mind, my hands, and my mouth. Teach me to love and humbly submit to your will. In Jesus's name I pray. Amen.

READ JAMES 4:13–5:12

I'm a planner. My calendar is color coded with six different colors. Before online calendars, I had a large, zippered, leather binder that I carried everywhere. I block out birthday weekends years in advance. I make reservations way ahead of time. I enjoy thinking ahead and making plans. If you're like me, you read James's words and wonder if this is the kind of planning that James condemns. If so, is the solution to simply tack the words, "Lord willing" at the end of each entry into my calendar? In some ways, that would be easier than what James is saying. As always, he's concerned with the posture of the heart—are we pridefully presumptuous or are we humbly dependent?

1. How does verse 16 help us understand the type of planning that James rebukes?

2. Do you think James wants us to say, "If the Lord wills" at the end of each sentence we speak or write?

    a. Why or why not?

    b. What does James want us to do?

You may be surprised, but the number one song played at funerals in America is *My Way* by Frank Sinatra.[19] The song lyrics are a soliloquy of a person glorying in all her seemingly self-sufficient accomplishments—she's laughed and cried, she's loved and lost, she's had doubts and regrets—but she's done it all her way. The irony of playing this song at a funeral is exactly the point James is making—our lives are but a mist, so who are we to be boastful in our self-determination? In fact, he says it's more than ironic, such boasting is evil.

3.   James likens our life to a mist in order to explain why we shouldn't be overconfident in our own abilities and plans. How would you describe a mist?

4.   One commentator offers three self-descriptive words to help guard our hearts against presumption: ignorance, frailty, and dependence.[20] Where do you see each (or any) of these described in verses 13–17?

·   *Ignorance*:

·   *Frailty*:

·   *Dependence*:

We don't like to think of ourselves as any of those! And yet, we are. We're ignorant of the future. We're frail, temporary beings. And we're utterly and completely dependent on the Lord for our next breath. Acknowledging these things puts us in a posture of right humility before the Lord. We aren't to think, "I'm going to do it my way." We're to think, "Show me *your* way, oh Lord."

As James begins his next section, he sounds more like an Old Testament prophet than a pastoral apostle. He comes out of the gates with harsh condemnation for the "rich." But, consistent with the rest of his letter, James isn't condemning wealth in and of itself. He is condemning the misuse of wealth and calling attention to sins that wealth can precipitate. As one commentator points out, there is no sin in being rich, the sin comes "in the way it is gained, the way it is used, and the spirit which it tends to engender in the heart."[21]

5. In today's world, our riches don't literally rot and our garments are rarely eaten by moths. How would you describe what James is talking about in modern language?

6. In what ways might these things serve as "evidence against [us]" (5:3)?

7. Put everything happening in verses 1–6 under one of the three headings below.

PAST: WHAT HAS ALREADY HAPPENED?	PRESENT: WHAT IS CURRENTLY HAPPENING?	FUTURE: WHAT WILL HAPPEN?

8. Who might fall in the category of "laborers who mowed your fields" in today's society or in your own life?

If James is speaking about wealthy unbelievers in verses 1–6, he might be speaking to the laborers who have been exploited in verses 7–11. He is encouraging them to patiently endure in the midst of injustice and trial, by reminding them of a few things: the Lord of hosts has heard their cry (verse 4), the Lord is coming back (verses 7 and 8), and the prophets and Job stand as examples of steadfastness in suffering.

9.   List all of the ways we can know James is speaking to believers in verses 7–11.

10.   As a reminder, circle any of the following words or phrases that could be synonymous with the word *steadfast*.

Enduring   Optimistic   Patient   Perseverant

Happy All the Time   Remaining   Holding Fast   Confident

11.   What are the similarities between verse 11 and what James said in the beginning of his letter, "Blessed is the man who remains steadfast under trial, for when he has stood the test he will receive the crown of life, which God has promised to those who love him" (1:12)?

12.   In verse 12, do you think James is more concerned about whether or not we take oaths or about what our speech reveals of our honesty and integrity. Why?

James has never been one to mince words, but he really comes on strongly in these verses—even for him! It's easy to read our passage for this week and wonder if all of our planning is sinful, all of our money is evil, and all of our promises are immoral. It's important to remember that James is coming after our heart attitudes in all of these things, and he's doing it so that we will be humble, resting, and steadfast in the Lord.

As you work on your memory verse for this week, don't lose heart! If the Lord is using his Word to convict or instruct you in a particular way, remember that it's his kindness that leads us to repentance (Rom. 2:4). He's accomplishing his purposes in us.

MEMORY VERSE

Behold, we consider those blessed who remained steadfast. You have heard of the steadfastness of Job, and you have seen the purpose of the Lord, how the Lord is compassionate and merciful.

James 5:11

DAY 3

Interpretation: What Do Other Scriptures Say?

◆

PRAY

Father, Jesus, and Spirit, I bow before you today keenly and painfully aware that I love myself more than I should and love you much less than I should. Show me times I don't submit to your plans, places I hoard and misuse the money you've given me, and scenarios when my words are untrustworthy. Cause my love for you to grow and cause my love of self and my possessions to diminish. I ask this in Jesus's name. Amen.

READ JAMES 4:13-5:12

The 1980 movie, *Fame*, is the story of high school students in New York City auditioning for a performing arts high school. Each student is an aspiring artist with dreams of "making it big." The title song is sung in a flash-mob style with students pouring out of the school into the street dancing and declaring that everyone listening should take note and remember their names because they're going to be famous—immortal even.

They have all the confidence and hope in the world that they have what it takes to receive all the fame and glory they desire. They've planned it all out and are entirely confident in their plans, their competence, and the worthiness of their goals.

It's this type of arrogant boasting that James is admonishing. It's not wrong to plan, it's wrong to think we're the masters of our own destiny. As James points out, we don't even have control over tomorrow, much less our whole lives.

1. Read Proverbs 16:3 and 16:9. What do you learn about planning? Are you to make plans? If so, what are you to do with them?

2. Read Proverbs 19:21. How does this help you think rightly about your plans?

As we saw yesterday, James helps us see that we're ignorant of the future, frail in the present, and dependent all the time.

3. Read the following verses and circle the word or words used to describe the brevity of life.

   · Hosea 13:3: Therefore they shall be like the morning mist or like the dew that goes early away, like the chaff that swirls from the threshing floor or like smoke from a window.

   · Ecclesiastes 6:12: For who knows what is good for man while he lives the few days of his vain life, which he passes like a shadow?

   · Job 7:7: Remember that my life is a breath; my eye will never again see good.

   · Psalm 39:5: Behold, you have made my days a few hand-breadths, and my lifetime is as nothing before you. Surely all mankind stands as a mere breath!

   · Psalm 90:5: You sweep them away as with a flood; they are like a dream, like grass that is renewed in the morning.

4. According to the following verses, what are we to boast in? How are each of these the polar opposite of what the world would have us boast in?

SCRIPTURE:	WHAT WE ARE TO BOAST IN:	WHAT THE WORLD TELLS US TO BOAST IN:
1 Corinthians 1:31: so that, as it is written, "Let the one who boasts, boast in the Lord."		
2 Corinthians 1:14: just as you did partially understand us—that on the day of our Lord Jesus you will boast of us as we will boast of you.		
2 Corinthians 11:30: If I must boast, I will boast of the things that show my weakness.		
Galatians 6:14: But far be it from me to boast except in the cross of our Lord Jesus Christ, by which the world has been crucified to me, and I to the world.		

5. Read Matthew 6:9–10 and 26:42. How can praying like this help you submit your plans to the Lord?

It's not just our plans we're to submit to the Lord, we're to submit our resources, too. Remember, James is not condemning the possession of wealth, he's denouncing the mishandling of it—specifically hoarding, withholding, and hedonistic spending. These are sins we're all capable of, but the possession of wealth puts us at higher risk for these particular sins. Job was a very wealthy man, but his steadfastness in suffering proved that his hope was not in his riches, it was in the Lord.

6. Read 1 Timothy 6:9–10. What are some ways riches can be a snare?

7. Read 1 Timothy 6:17–19.

    a. Where are the rich not to set their hope and why?

    b. What are they to be rich in?

    c. How does this tie into what James has already said in his letter?

8.   Read Deuteronomy 24:14–15.

   a.   When are you to give wages earned? Why?

   b.   What does Moses call it if you don't?

   c.   Who might be considered "a hired worker . . . whether he
        is one of your brothers or one of the sojourners . . . in your
        land" in our cultural context today?

9.   Read Leviticus 19:9–10 and 13.

   a.   What did God want the Israelites to leave and why?

   b.   What two words does God call withholding wages for
        even a night?

10. Read the following parable from Luke 12:15–20.

   And he said to them, "Take care, and be on your guard against
   all covetousness, for one's life does not consist in the abun-
   dance of his possessions." And he told them a parable, saying,
   "The land of a rich man produced plentifully, and he thought to

himself, 'What shall I do, for I have nowhere to store my crops?' And he said, 'I will do this: I will tear down my barns and build larger ones, and there I will store all my grain and my goods. And I will say to my soul, "Soul, you have ample goods laid up for many years; relax, eat, drink, be merry."' But God said to him, 'Fool! This night your soul is required of you, and the things you have prepared, whose will they be?'

a. What do we learn about the relationship between the amount of the man's harvest and his need?

b. What could the man have done with his crops besides store them?

c. What does Jesus say he did instead?

d. What are modern day ways we "build bigger barns to store our surplus?"

e. Write down as many correlations as you can between this parable and the thoughts of James in 4:13–17 and 5:1–6?

11. I Peter 1:13 says, "Therefore, preparing your minds for action, and being sober-minded, set your hope fully on the grace that will be brought to you at the revelation of Jesus Christ."

    a.   Where are we to set our hope?

    b.   When will that hope be fulfilled?

    c.   How is that similar to what James said in 5:8?

12. Job 19:25–26 says, "For I know that my Redeemer lives, and at the last he will stand upon the earth. And after my skin has been thus destroyed, yet in my flesh I shall see God."

    a.   What was Job's hope?

    b.   How do you think that hope made him steadfast?

As you work on your memory verse, ask the Lord to meet you in your suffering and give you a steadfast faith like Job and the prophets. Meditate on the Lord's compassion and mercy in your own life as you rehearse this verse today.

MEMORY VERSE

*Behold, we consider those blessed who remained
steadfast. You have heard of the steadfastness of
Job, and you have seen the purpose of the Lord,
how the Lord is compassionate and merciful.*

James 5:11

DAY 4

Application: How Does the Text Transform Me?

♦

PRAY

Father, at times it's hard to sit under the weight of your Word. I ask
that you help me to stay here and not run away from the weight too
quickly. Remind me that conviction is a mercy and it's your kindness
that leads me to repentance. Thank you for your faithfulness to me.
In Jesus's name I pray. Amen.

READ JAMES 4:13–5:12

When my children were small, my husband and I built a house in
the country. I loved that house and I loved living in the country. I
told people, "My girls are going to get married under those trees"

and "This is the house my grandchildren will come to visit" and "I'm going to die in this house."

We sold that house in 2009 and moved to St. Louis to go to seminary. Of course I *knew* the bold statements I had made depended on the Lord's way and will, but it would have been better for my heart to have verbally acknowledged that—not as a talisman, but as a reminder of my dependence on the Lord. As one commentator says, "To be sure the words 'If the Lord wills' can be a protective superstition; but they can also be the sweetest and most comfortable reassurance to a humble and trustful spirit."[22]

1.   Make a list of 2–3 plans you are currently making.

     a.   In what ways have you submitted those plans to the Lord?

     b.   What are your hopes in each of your plans?

     c.   Next to each, write a prayer asking the Lord to show you his will and help you submit to it.

2.   What is the difference between asking the Lord to show you his plan and asking him to bless the plans you've already made?

3.   James says in verse 17, "Whoever knows the right thing to do
     and fails to do it, for him it is sin."

     a.   What are 3–4 things God has revealed in James's letter so
          far that are "the right thing to do"?

     b.   Next to each, write down if you're doing them and,
          if so, how.

     c.   What are some right things you know you're to do, that
          you're currently not doing?

As we've already said, the beginning of chapter 5 contains some of
the toughest words in James's entire letter. The temptation is to be
consoled by thinking that James was speaking about unbelievers.
But that consolation shouldn't lead us to dismiss his admonishments
as inapplicable to us. In fact, just the opposite! If unbelievers are
rebuked for hoarding money and exploiting people in this way, *how
much more so* for a believer? We can't skirt out from under these
verses too quickly.

4.   Spend a few minutes prayerfully asking the Lord to show you:

     a.   where you have left (or could leave) margin in your
          resources.

b. how you have "laid up" resources in a way that indicates either hoarding or self-indulgence.

c. what the "evidence" of your resources says about you.

d. ways you can faithfully steward what he's given you.

5. In what ways are you tempted to trust in wealth rather than in Christ?

6. Do you identify more with the "rich," the "laborers," or with both (5:1–6)? Why?

7. Write down one tangible way to use the resources you've been given to care for others.

James returns to a topic he began his letter with—suffering, and how we are to respond. In chapter 1, we're told to be steadfast in our various trials because we will receive the crown of life (1:12). As we near the end of the letter, we're told to be patient because the coming of the Lord is at hand. Patience and steadfastness are related, but aren't synonymous. Where patience sits back and waits, steadfastness is more of an active endurance.

8.   Describe a trial that required you to be patient. How could thinking about the Lord's return help you be patient in your suffering?

One commentator says that James is trying to convey to his readers that, "Your present suffering . . . is not the 'end' of the story; God will transform your situation for good when Christ is revealed in glory."[23] In other words, hang in there! As Paul said, "For I consider that the sufferings of this present time are not worth comparing with the glory that is to be revealed to us" (Rom. 8:18). It's not that our present suffering isn't significant or seen by our loving Father, it's that, one day, our suffering will be fully ended, redeemed, and made right. Until that day, James wants us to be patient and steadfast in our very real sufferings.

9.   James gives us the prophets and Job as examples of patience and steadfastness in suffering. Who has been an example to you in the way they've suffered? How has their response to suffering encouraged and strengthened you?

Throughout his letter, James has said a lot about our words. He's told us not to say that God is tempting us (1:13); we're to be slow to speak (1:19) and bridle our tongues (1:26); we aren't to verbally profess a faith that isn't backed by deeds of faith (2:14); we're to recognize that our tongue can be a restless evil, causing much damage (3:1–12); and we're not to slander (4:11), boast (4:16), or grumble (5:9). He now comes to the end of his inventory of sins of the tongue—swearing on something greater than ourselves in order to validate the truth of our words. As he said in 3:10, this "ought not to be so."

James is addressing more than just oaths in verse 12. He's admonishing his readers not to have "loopholes" in our agreements, or carefully crafted promises so we can wiggle out of our word. We're not to tell "white lies," even to avoid hurting a friend's feelings or to get out of a sticky situation. We're not to mislead others in any way!

10. In what ways do you struggle to be honest in your speech? Are you prone to exaggeration, white lies, or half-truths?

11. Describe the last time it was hard for you to be a woman of your word.

    a. Can you identify why it was difficult? What was the desire that waged war within you?

    b. How has James helped you want to pursue being a seamlessly honest person?

    c. What is one way you can act on your conviction?

As we sit under God's Word and realize that our plans can be arrogant, our money can be hoarded, and our words can be false, we need both humility and wisdom to change. Praise God that he's the one who gives both. When we humble ourselves, he will give more grace (4:6), and when we ask for wisdom, he gives generously without reproach (1:5). Humble yourself before the Lord and trust that he's conforming you more into the image of Jesus.

MEMORY VERSE

Behold, we consider those blessed who remained steadfast. You have heard of the steadfastness of Job, and you have seen the purpose of the Lord, how the Lord is compassionate and merciful.

James 5:11

DAY 5

Reflection

◆

Have you ever wondered what God's will is for your life? I'd venture to guess that we've all asked that question at some point. For most of us, the question rises to the surface at critical junctures in our lives: choosing a spouse or a job, choosing what school to attend or which house to buy. These are the times we tend to ask, "Lord, what is your will for my life?"

There's a tension most of us feel in seeking to know God's will. For some, it becomes an unbiblical pursuit, seeking to know his will through horoscopes, signs, or unusual coincidences. Others swing to the opposite end, thinking that God doesn't really care about the details of their lives and he surely doesn't have a "will" for anything they do.

As we saw in James's letter this week, it's good to acknowledge our dependence on the Lord's will. We're to submit to it, saying, "If the Lord wills, we will live and do this or that" (4:15). But how are we to know if the Lord wills something or not?

It's helpful to recognize that theologians discuss God's one will in two primary ways—his secret will and his revealed will. His secret will (sometimes referred to as his hidden or decretive will) refers to the fact that God is sovereign and rules over all things. Nothing happens outside of God's perfect will. It's called hidden or secret because we don't know what his will is until it has come to pass. God told Isaiah, "I am God, and there is no other; I am God, and there is none like me, declaring the end from the beginning and from ancient times things not yet done, saying, 'My counsel shall stand, and I will accomplish all my purpose'" (Isa. 46:9–10). This is the sovereign, but hidden, will of God and nothing will thwart it.

God's revealed will is that which he has made known to us in his Word. For instance, we know it's God's will for us to love our neighbors, bridle our tongues, act justly, love mercy, and walk humbly. We know it's God's will that we not murder, steal, cheat, lie, slander, gossip, or boast. How do we know? Because he has told us explicitly in his Word. In fact, it can hardly be said more clearly than in 1 Thessalonians 4:3, "For this is the will of God, your sanctification."

Ironically, we're prone to minimize God's revealed will and hyper-focus on his secret will. Many times, we want to know God's hidden will for the future, while we walk contrary to his revealed will in the present. Instead, we should trust in God's providence—that

ıe works all things together for the good of those who believe (Rom.
3:28)—while obeying his revealed will.

However, it can be difficult to trust in God's plan, especially
during trials. We think that suffering can't possibly be the Lord's will.
We forget that our salvation was won when Jesus submitted himself
completely to God's will in the moment of his greatest suffering.

After living a life of perfect obedience to God's revealed will,
Jesus, on the night before his crucifixion, asked his Father three
times if there was any other way for him to accomplish God's plan
to save a people for himself. Everything hinged on how Jesus would
respond to God's perfect will. And, praise and glory to the Son, Jesus
submitted himself, saying, "Your will be done" (Matt. 26:42).

So how are we to respond to the will of the Lord? Be diligent
in obeying God's revealed will. Walk in holiness, pursue sanctification, love our neighbors, be generous with our resources, bridle
our tongues, and worship God. Trust that God, in his providence,
is working all things together for our good; and what we currently
cannot see will one day be revealed in glory. As we wait with steadfast hope for that day, thank the Lord that his will is good.

1. Take five minutes to summarize what you've learned this week
    and then use those thoughts to journal and guide your prayer.

2. Try to write the memory verse for this week's chapter, without
    looking at it!

GROUP DISCUSSION QUESTIONS

◆

ICEBREAKER: What's your favorite thing to plan (dinner, a party, a business strategy, an interior design, etc.)?

WARM-UP: What is one thing you're in the midst of planning right now?

Have someone (or several people) read James 4:13–5:12 out loud.

1. Describe a time your plans were thwarted, but you see now how the Lord was redirecting you.

2. Are you more of a "planner" or do you tend to "go with the flow"? In what ways are James's words relevant to all of us?

3. What effect has thinking about the brevity of life had on you this week?

4. Name something you tend to hoard. How has our passage this week instructed you?

5. James has had a lot to say in his letter about the misuse of money. What has been the most convicting for you regarding money?

6. How is thinking of God as the Commander of heaven's armies and the Defender of the defenseless either comforting or challenging to you?

7. How does the reminder that the Lord is coming again help you remain patient in trials?

8. Why do you think James says, "We consider those blessed who remained steadfast?"

9. If you're willing, share with your group a way you are going to pursue being a woman of your word, letting your "yes" be yes and your "no" be no.

10. What was one thing that stood out/convicted/encouraged/instructed you this week?

CHAPTER 7

Steadfast Prayer: Trusting Our Faithful God

◆

JAMES 5:13–20

(13) Is anyone among you suffering? Let him pray. Is anyone cheerful? Let him sing praise. (14) Is anyone among you sick? Let him call for the elders of the church, and let them pray over him, anointing him with oil in the name of the Lord. (15) And the prayer of faith will save the one who is sick, and the Lord will raise him up. And if he has committed sins, he will be forgiven. (16) Therefore, confess your sins to one another and pray for one another, that you may be healed. The prayer of a righteous person has great power as it is working. (17) Elijah was a man with a nature like ours, and he prayed fervently that it might not rain, and for three years and six months it did not rain on the earth. (18) Then he prayed again, and heaven gave rain, and the earth bore its fruit.

(19) My brothers*, if anyone among you wanders from the truth and someone brings him back, (20) let him know that whoever brings back a sinner from his wandering will save his soul from death and will cover a multitude of sins.

* Or "brothers and sisters". The Greek word *adelphoi* is plural and can refer to both men and women who are siblings in the spiritual family of God.

DAY 1

Observation: What Does the Text Say?

◆

PRAY

Father, I bow before you and your Word today. You're God alone, the One who knows both the beginning and end of all things. Help me to trust you in all things, love you in all things, submit to you in all things, and glorify you in all things. I ask this in Jesus's name. Amen.

READ JAMES 5:13–20 (IF POSSIBLE, READ IT OUT LOUD.)

Remember, today is the day we just observe the text and ask questions like *who, what, when, where, why,* and *how*.

1.   Go back through the text:

   a.   Mark any words or phrases that stand out to you. Make note of patterns, key phrases, and repeated words.

   b.   Write in the margin two to three things that stand out or questions you might have.

I'm guessing we all had some questions as we read the verses above! If last week's passage contained some of James's most challenging words, this week's passage might contain some of his most perplexing. For any of us who've prayed for a friend or loved one to be healed of an illness, and they weren't, these verses can be more than perplexing—they can be painful. My hope is that, as we slow down and spend time seeking to understand what James is saying, we'll not only grow in our knowledge of God's Word, but that God himself will meet, comfort, and strengthen us through his living Word.

2.   According to verses 13–14:

   a.   What should the suffering person do?

   b.   What should the cheerful person do?

   c.   What should the sick person do?

   d.   What two things are the elders to do?

   e.   In whose name is this to be done?

3.   How many times is praying or prayer mentioned in verses 13–18?

James mentions the prayers of the suffering and the cheerful (verse 13), the prayers of the elders (verse 14), the prayer of faith (verse 15), prayers for each other (verse 16), the prayer of the righteous (verse 16), and the prayers of Elijah (verses 17–18). According to these verses, Christians should pray in times of suffering, sickness, and sin. We should pray for ourselves, our brothers and sisters, and those under our care. If we only take one thing away from our study this week, let it be that God wants his children to come to him in prayer at all times, in all seasons, and for all reasons. We're to be steadfast in prayer.

4. Regarding the prayer for the sick person:

    a. Who is to pray for whom?

    b. Who is praying the "prayer of faith"?

    c. According to verse 15, what three things "will" happen?

    _____ will _____.

    _____ will _____.

    _____ will _____.

This verse can be difficult to read and even more challenging to understand. If we pray for healing (for ourselves or others) and don't receive it, it's easy to wonder if we didn't "do it right" (i.e. we didn't have enough faith or we didn't pray the "right prayer") or if God didn't "come through" on his Word. Of course, neither of those can be true. God's actions are not dependent on the amount of faith we have, nor does our faith obligate God to do something outside of his sovereign and good will. It's not as if God's plan becomes subservient to our wishes if only we can attain a certain amount of faith. As one commentator says, "Healing is a gift, not a reward . . . It is a mistake to congratulate ourselves for strong faith when God grants a request and a mistake to blame ourselves when he refuses one."[24]

So how are we to understand what James is saying? Well, it's going to take us all week to faithfully seek understanding and apply these truths. Today, we're only observing and trying to ask good questions of the text.

5.   Read verse 16.

    a.   What two things are we supposed to do with one another?

    b.   What does James say will be the result?

    c.   What kind of person has powerful prayers?

6.   How is Elijah described and how did he pray?

7.   What two things did Elijah pray for?

The entire letter of James has been direct and to-the-point. James doesn't mince or waste words. The ending of his letter is no different. There is no benediction, doxology, or mention of names of anyone he wishes to thank. He ends his letter the same way he has written throughout—passionately concerned that his readers live out their faith.

8.   How does James address his readers one last time (verse 19)?

9.   Describe the scenario in verses 19–20.

As you work on your memory verse for this week, remember that James has written extensively on what the individual believer should and shouldn't do. But, throughout his letter, he has also been concerned with the community of believers—how we care for one another, speak to and about one another, honor one another, serve one another, and pray for one another. James knows that we are, in fact, our brothers' and sisters' keepers.

MEMORY VERSE

Therefore, confess your sins to one another and pray for one another, that you may be healed. The prayer of a righteous person has great power as it is working.

James 5:16

DAY 2

Interpretation: What Does the Text Mean?

◆

PRAY

Father, Son, and Holy Spirit, I confess that I don't turn to you in prayer as often or as quickly as I should. Teach me how to pray in all seasons and for all reasons; teach me to pray for my brothers and sisters; teach me what it means to pray in your name. Thank you that you welcome me into your presence. I ask this in Jesus's name. Amen.

READ JAMES 5:13-20

James begins and ends his letter on the subject of suffering. In chapter 1, he exhorts his readers to respond to trials and suffering with joy because we're to know that suffering will produce something good and right and beautiful in us—steadfastness and spiritual maturity. As we near the end of his letter, James wants his readers to know that as we encounter these various types of trials and suffering, our first response should be to pray.

1. In what ways might prayer be related to the steadfastness James talks about in 1:2?

2. How is singing praise a type of prayer?

James moves from general suffering to a specific type of suffering—serious physical illness. The sick person described in these verses is most likely sick enough to be confined to home, if not to bed. This is evidenced by the fact that the elders need to come to her, and furthermore, that she needs to be prayed *over* and raised *up*. This helps us understand the particular type of suffering James has in mind here.

3.   According to verse 14, list the sequence of events.

4.   In what ways might the phrase "in the name of the Lord" (verse 14) be related to the "prayer of faith" in verse 15?

Yesterday, we looked at the three things James says "will" happen: the prayer of faith *will* save, the Lord *will* raise the sick person up, and the sick person *will* be forgiven. In verse 16, James says that, as we confess to and pray for one another, we *may* be healed.

5.   To the best of your ability, write a few words that explain what each of the following might mean.

    ·   Saved:
    ·   Raised up:
    ·   Forgiven:
    ·   Healed:

In order to best understand these verses, it's very important to remember what James has already written. In our passage last week, we saw that we're a mist that vanishes and our very lives are completely dependent on the will of the Lord.

6.   Turn back and read James 4:14–15.

   a.   How does 4:14–15 help you understand 5:14–15?

   b.   If every life is "a mist that appears for a little while and then vanishes," what comfort does that offer when our prayers for healing are not granted?

When James tells us to "pray in the name of the Lord" we're to remember what he's already told us about the Lord, our lives, and prayer:

   ·   We're to ask in faith, without doubt, knowing that God gives generously to all without reproach (1:5–6).

   ·   Every good and perfect gift is from above, coming down from the Father of lights (1:17).

   ·   We're to submit ourselves to and humble ourselves before the Lord (4:7, 10).

   ·   There is only one who is able to save and destroy (4:11).

   ·   We're a mist that appears for a little while and then vanishes (4:14).

·   We're to be patient until the coming of the Lord; the com-
     ing of the Lord is at hand (5:8–9).

·   The Lord is compassionate and merciful (5:11).

God gives good gifts, of which physical healing is one. The prayer of
faith means going to the Lord, believing he *can* heal, asking him *to*
heal, and trusting him whether he does or doesn't heal.

     Every one of us, because our life is a mist, will face the day that
physical healing will not come. And yet, for those of us who are in
the Lord we *will* be raised up; we *will* be saved; and we *will* be eter-
nally healed. The Lord is faithful to his Word.

7.   In verse 16, James links forgiveness of sins with physical healing.

     a.   Is physical illness ever a result of sin? Give examples.

     b.   Is physical illness always a result of sin? Why or why not?

8.   What do you think James means when he writes, "The prayer of
     a righteous person has great power as it is working"?

James went out of his way to let us know that Elijah "was a man
with a nature like ours" and his prayers were effective. In this entire
passage, the focus is on the prayer of the ordinary person—the believer, the elder, the friend, and Elijah. When James calls attention
to the prayer of the "righteous," we need to know that James isn't

saying there are some super-Christians out there whose prayers are more powerful than the rest of ours. We need to go back to James's discussion on justification and righteousness (chapter 3) and recall that *everyone* who is in Christ has been declared righteous. James isn't talking about some "super-saints"—you and I are the righteous ones whose prayers have great power as they are working!

The last thought on James's mind as he closes his letter, is the brother or sister who has wandered from the faith. The person he describes is someone who has been in the church but has walked away. Maybe they've just stopped coming to church. Maybe they're living a life contrary to the Word of God. Or maybe they're blatantly denying their faith. There are a lot of ways to wander.

The word James uses for *wanders* is the same word he used in 1:16 that is translated *deceived*.

9.   Read James 1:14–16. How might being deceived be related to wandering?

10. List at least three ways that someone can wander from the truth.

As you work on your memory verse today, ask the Lord to keep you from being deceived and wandering from the truth. At the same time, ask him to help you boldly pray for and pursue your brothers and sisters who are wandering. In Christ, your prayers are powerful and effective.

DAY 3

Interpretation: What Do Other Scriptures Say?

◆

PRAY

Father, thank you that you hear my prayers. As I come to your Word today, I ask you, Holy Spirit, to open my eyes to see, my ears to hear, my mind to comprehend, and my heart to respond. Teach me to seek you, your will, and your ways in all things. I ask this in Jesus's name. Amen.

READ JAMES 5:13–20

I have a child who has the ability to (dangerously) hyper-focus. As a small child, if she saw something across the street or parking lot that captured her attention, she would dash towards it without ever stopping to see if any cars were coming. Whatever held her interest kept her from seeing the bigger picture. We can sometimes do the same thing as we read Scripture. I don't want that to be true of us as we study this passage.

The big picture in this passage is that God wants us, welcomes us, and invites us to come to him in prayer in all circumstances—when we're suffering, joyful, sick, in sin, and in need. He wants us to pray when our faith is weak and when our faith is strong. He wants us to pray fervently, frequently, and faithfully. Regardless of the questions you might have about this text, don't lose sight of the glorious truth that our Lord desires us to come to him in prayer, in all things.

1.   Read 1 Thessalonians 5:17–18. Give an example of how we can "give thanks in all circumstances" when we're:

    ·   Suffering (James 5:13)

    ·   Cheerful (James 5:13)

    ·   Sick (James 5:14)

Two of the big questions for our passage this week revolve around the role of faith in healing and sin in sickness. Is healing dependent on the amount of our faith? And is illness the result of our sin? Let's tackle the first of these questions.

2.   Read the following passages:

And he said to her, "Daughter, your faith has made you well; go in peace, and be healed of your disease." (Mark 5:34)

They said to him, "Lord, let our eyes be opened." And Jesus in pity touched their eyes, and immediately they recovered their sight and followed him. (Matthew 20:33–34)

    a.   In Mark 5, what is the basis given for her healing?

    b.   In Matthew 20, what is the basis given for their healing?

3.   Read Luke 7:47–50. What does Jesus say to the woman?

The words "your faith has made you well" and "your faith has saved you" are exactly the same words in the Greek—and the same ones James uses. There's the sense that both physical and spiritual healing are in view. The words James uses (i.e. save, raised up, forgiven, and healed) have both a physical and spiritual reality to them. God is not at all *un*concerned with our need for physical healing; but our greatest need is spiritual healing. We need to be forgiven, restored, justified, and healed so that we'll be raised up on the last day.

In 2 Corinthians, the apostle Paul tells us that he asked God to remove the "thorn in his flesh" (most scholars think this was a physical ailment). Paul was asking to be healed.

4.   Read 2 Corinthians 12:7–9.

    a.   What word is used to describe how Paul prayed?

    b.   How many times did he ask?

c.   How did the Lord answer him?

d.   What insight does this give you into our James passage?

Even Paul didn't receive what he asked for in prayer. If this doesn't convince you that the answer to your prayer isn't dependent on the strength of your faith, then remember the passage we looked at last week. In Matthew 26 we saw that Jesus, too, asked the Father three times to take something from him. And the Father said no. Oh, sisters, please know that if the Father has not given you the healing you've pleaded for, it's not because your faith is too small. God is not limited by our limited faith.

5.   Read Ephesians 3:20 and fill in the blanks:

[God] is able to do _____ _____ abundantly than all that we _____ or _____.

Does this mean we don't need to go to God in prayer, asking, pleading even, for what we think is best? No! Paul asked. Jesus asked. We're to go to God in all things with great faith. This faith simultaneously knows that God can heal, but humbly acknowledges that God knows best and will do what's best—even better than anything we can think or ask.

Our faith can't be in ourselves, thinking we know best. Our faith can't even be in our faith or in our ability to pray. Our faith always has to be grounded in the perfect, sovereign, and good will of God, trusting that he "is so generous that he will withhold nothing from us that is good."[25]

Now, onto our second big question: Is James saying that illness is a result of sin? Hopefully you saw in the homework yesterday that some illnesses *are* a direct result of sin—but most are not.

6. Compare the following passages from John's gospel.

JOHN 5:5–9, 14	JOHN 9:2–3, 6–7
(5) One man was there who had been an invalid for thirty-eight years. (6) When Jesus saw him lying there and knew that he had already been there a long time, he said to him, "Do you want to be healed?" … (8) Jesus said to him, "Get up, take up your bed, and walk." (9) And at once the man was healed, and he took up his bed and walked. … (14) Afterward Jesus found him in the temple and said to him, "See, you are well! Sin no more, that nothing worse may happen to you."	1) As he passed by, he saw a man blind from birth. (2) And his disciples asked him, "Rabbi, who sinned, this man or his parents, that he was born blind?" (3) Jesus answered, "It was not that this man sinned, or his parents, but that the works of God might be displayed in him. … (6) Having said these things, he spit on the ground and made mud with the saliva. Then he anointed the man's eyes with the mud (7) and said to him, "Go, wash in the pool of Siloam" (which means Sent). So he went and washed and came back seeing.

a. What do you learn about the connection between sin and illness?

b. What did Jesus do for both men?

Some illnesses are a direct result of sin. Others are a result of the fact that we live in a world in which everything's broken, including our bodies. James simply wants us to take the time to ask God if our sickness is a result of our sin. If so, we're to confess, having the faith to know that we will be forgiven.

7. Read Matthew 9:2–6.

    a. What does Jesus do about the man's sin?

    b. What does Jesus do about his illness?

    c. Which one was greater?

As James concludes his letter, he instructs his readers that the church should not only gather to pray for physical healing (verses 14–16), but that the church should certainly gather to pray for and pursue those needing spiritual healing—the ones who have wandered (verses 19–20).

8. Read the following verses and write down what you learn about *when*, *how*, and *why* we're to pursue our wandering brothers and sisters.

    a. *How* are we to restore our wandering siblings?

Galatians 6:1: Brothers, if anyone is caught in any transgression, you who are spiritual should restore him in a spirit of gentleness. Keep watch on yourself, lest you too be tempted.

b.   *When* are we to exhort each other?

Hebrews 3:13: But exhort one another every day, as long as it is called "today," that none of you may be hardened by the deceitfulness of sin.

c.   *Why* are we to pursue transgressors?

Psalm 51:13: Then I will teach transgressors your ways, and sinners will return to you.

Remember that the big picture in this week's passage is that the Lord wants us to come to him in prayer at all times. As you work on your memory verse today, ask the Lord to show you things to pray for (joys, sins, others, sickness, etc.) that you normally don't pray about.

MEMORY VERSE

Therefore, confess your sins to one another and pray for one another, that you may be healed. The prayer of a righteous person has great power as it is working.

James 5:16

DAY 4

Application: How Does the Text Transform Me?

◆

PRAY

Almighty God, I ask that you would use your Word today to teach me and transform me more into the image of your precious Son. Teach me to pray, but, most of all, teach me to trust. I ask this in Jesus's name. Amen.

READ JAMES 5:13-20

Most of us don't have trouble obeying the imperatives in James 5:13 to pray when suffering and sing praises when cheerful. During times of suffering, even unbelievers turn to God in prayer, and cheerfulness and joy can easily cause us to hum, whistle, and sing praises to God. But it's verse 14 that can, in our modern world, be hard to obey. Oh, we ask for prayer when we're sick, but James doesn't just tell us to pray. He tells us to call our elders and have them come to us, pray over us, and anoint us with oil. For many, James's commands feel outdated and odd.

1. List some things that can hinder us from calling our elders to come to us, pray over us, and anoint us with oil when we're seriously sick?

    a. Which of these would be the biggest hinderance for you? Why?

    b. What are you most likely to do when faced with a serious illness?

2. Thinking about last week's Reflection section, what in verse 14 would fall under God's revealed will? What would be part of his secret will?

I'm going to venture a guess that many of us are unsure about why James would tell us to be anointed with oil. Some tend to be almost superstitious about it, thinking that the oil itself has some magical quality. Others think it's archaic and want to have nothing to do with it. However, James includes it in his instructions on what we should do when we are very sick, so we need a biblical understanding of it. I find Doriani's comments most helpful:

The anointing is not a sacrament, but it can symbolize the power of the Holy Spirit. By this anointing, the church's leaders set apart the sick person for special attention, even healing, from God. This does not displace physicians . . . Anointing is neither magical nor sacramental, but it is quasi-sacramental. Like other solemn ceremonies such as weddings or ordinations, the ceremony makes us pause so that we take the action seriously. [26]

Even when we take prayer seriously, every one of us will, one day, not receive the physical healing we ask for, unless Jesus comes back first. But, until that day, we're to ask for it. We're to pray in faith that God is good, able, and wise and trust that his answer to our prayer will be in line with these things.

3. How might this week's lesson offer us comfort or hope when we pray for healing (for ourselves or someone else) and don't receive it?

James tells us that we're to confess our sins to one another. But this requires wisdom and discernment as we seek to obey. All sins need to be confessed to God. But, as we confess to each other, some sins need to be confessed to the person against whom we have sinned (e.g. stealing, lying, slander), while some sins are better off confessed to a third party (e.g. lust, bitterness, envy). As one commentator says, "It is highly unlikely that we will accomplish anything constructive by telling someone, 'I envied you,' or 'I lusted after you.'"[27]

The enemy knows that sin grows in darkness. He loves to keep us alone and isolated, "private" about our sin. That's one reason there's such great power in confessing our sins to one another. So, confess your sin to God, and ask him for the wisdom required to know who else you should confess to.

4. According to verse 16, what happens after we confess our sins to one another?

    a. Have you ever experienced the power of confessing your sin to someone and having them pray for you? If so, describe what it was like.

    b. Is there a sin you need to confess to someone else? If so, would it be more helpful to confess to the person who's the object of that sin or to someone else? Why?

    c. How should you respond if someone confesses a sin to you?

We've seen this week that we're to pray fervently, frequently, and for all things. We're to pray for ourselves and for each other.

5. Think about your prayer life. What are some ways you would like to grow in prayerfulness?

6. James describes a church where the members are intimately involved in each other's lives—praying for, confessing to, and pursuing each other.

a. Are you this connected to your church family? If not, how can you be more connected?

7. Do you tend to think that there are some "super-Christians" out there whose prayers are more powerful than yours? Why or why not?

a. How does 1 John 5:14—"And this is the confidence that we have toward him, that if we ask anything according to his will he hears us."—further explain what James is saying in verse 16?

b. What comfort is there in knowing he hears us, even if he doesn't heal us?

In the introduction of this study, I said that reading James is a bit like riding in the back of my mom's station wagon during a carpool ride—full of rapid soundbites of practical and relevant wisdom, covering a wide variety of topics. And James ends his letter in much the same way my mom would end our carpool rides: quickly stating some last words before I would hop out of the car. She might say, "Turn in your homework" or "Hope the math test goes well" or, more in line with James's last words, "Don't forget your brother."

8. Do you know anyone who has either stopped coming to church or started living contrary to the gospel?

    a. What are some practical things you can do to "bring them back"?

    b. What might hinder you from pursuing them?

9. The wandering brother and sister can be caught in a multitude of sins. Considering what James has already said about what we're *not* to do (i.e. slander, judge, show partiality, curse others) and what we *are* to do (i.e. love our neighbor, bridle our tongues, be doers of the Word), what are some ways we can "cover a multitude of sins" for our wandering brothers and sisters?

    a. Remembering the difference between discernment and judging (ch. 5, pg. 149), what does "covering a multitude of sins" not mean?

    b. Why is this important?

James has laid out some radical things for us to do. Calling the elders to come to us to pray and anoint us with oil may feel strange or unusual, depending upon your church background. Pursuing people when they walk away from the truth is not comfortable, or even socially acceptable, in many circles. But James has, throughout his letter, been calling us to steadfast obedience.

As you work on your memory verse, ask the Lord to give you a greater love for your brothers and sisters, showing you what it looks like to pray for, confess to, and go after them. May we love each other with the radical love of Christ.

MEMORY VERSE

Therefore, confess your sins to one another and pray for one another, that you may be healed. The prayer of a righteous person has great power as it is working.

James 5:16

DAY 5

Reflection

♦

James ends his letter with the words, "My brothers, if anyone among you wanders from the truth and someone brings him back, let him know that whoever brings back a sinner from his wandering will save his soul from death and will cover a multitude of sins." I have to wonder if James was thinking about his older Brother—the One who came, brought him back, saved his soul, and covered over a multitude of his sins. Because James, like all of us, was a wanderer.

All of humanity wanders. From the moment Adam and Eve were exiled out of Eden, humanity has been in a state of wandering. Because of sin, we're born as exiles, a people without a true home. And, unless we're rescued, we live our entire lives directionless, never knowing our true purpose. We wander around, wander away, and wander off.

But praise be to God, we have a Brother who saw our wandering plight and came to bring us back and save our souls. The author of Hebrews tells us that, in order to rescue us, the Son of God "had to be made like his brothers in every respect" (Heb. 2:17)—every respect, that is, except sin. He's our sinless older Brother, sent to bring us back to his Father.

This great rescue required Jesus to sacrifice and suffer. Paul tells us that Jesus, "who, though he was in the form of God, did not count equality with God a thing to be grasped, but *emptied himself*, by *taking the form of a servant*, being born in the likeness of men. And being found in human form, he *humbled himself* by becoming obedient to the point of death, even death on a cross" (Phil. 2:6–8, emphasis mine). Our older Brother gave up everything to come get us.

My husband, Craig, is the youngest child in his family. There are numerous stories told of times his older brother, Brian, stepped in to defend him from various bullies and neighborhood enemies. Our two great enemies are sin and death. Thankfully, our older Brother came to defeat them both on our behalf, by taking on the one who holds their power. The author of Hebrews tells us that Jesus became our brother so "that through death he might destroy the one who has the power of death, that is, the devil" (Heb. 2:14). But our older Brother didn't simply fight our enemies, he defeated them by laying down his life for us. It took his death to defeat death for us.

With the battle won, our Brother covers us. He knows we're na-
ked, ashamed, isolated, and covered in sin. He cleanses us of all our
unrighteousness (1 John 1:9) and covers us with his righteousness
(2 Cor. 5:21). And if our sin has been covered, we should join with
David in proclaiming, "Blessed is the one whose transgression is forgiven, whose sin is covered" (Ps. 32:1). Blessed indeed.

James knew that his older Brother had sacrificed much, suffered much, accomplished much, loved much, and forgiven much.
He wants us, his readers, to live our lives in response to the fact
that we're no longer wanderers—we've been rescued, brought
back, saved, and covered by our glorious older Brother, the Lord
Jesus Christ.

1. Take five minutes to summarize what you've learned this week
    and then use those thoughts to journal and guide your prayer.

2. Try to write the memory verse for this week's chapter, without
    looking at it!

GROUP DISCUSSION QUESTIONS

◆

ICEBREAKER: What do you sing when you're cheerful?

WARM-UP: When was the last time someone told you they were praying for you? How did it make you feel?

Have someone (or several people) read James 5:13–20 out loud.

1. Are you more likely to pray when you're suffering or when you're cheerful?

2. What are some reasons people might not call the elders to come, pray over them, and anoint them with oil?

3. Have you ever called the elders to pray over you? If you're comfortable sharing, what prompted it and what was the result?

4. Share one area in which you'd like to trust the Lord more. Write down what others share and pray for one another this week.

5. Why are some sins so much easier to confess publicly than others?

6. What keeps us from confessing our sins to each other?

7. James tells us that Elijah was a man with a nature like ours. How does this encourage you to pray with both boldness and humility?

8. How do James's assumptions about the connectedness of church members challenge you? How connected are you with others in your church?

9. How can we, as a church, do a better job of helping those who are wandering from the truth? What does it look like to do that well?

10. What was one thing that stood out/convicted/encouraged/instructed you this week?

Steadfast Review: Putting It All Together

◆

We've spent seven weeks together studying the book of James. I wish I were sitting around a table with you, hearing the insights, encouragements, and lessons you've learned from this book. Because, if you're like me, James has instructed, inspired, and challenged me over and over again!

This week, we're going to bring it all together, by looking back through the book of James and over our homework. Read the book in its entirety one last time. You can either read it through in one sitting or read one chapter each day before you answer the questions. There are just two questions each day, but they will require you to reflect on what the Lord has been teaching you. There's great benefit in reviewing and summarizing. At the end of Day 5, there's a place for you to "test" yourself on your memory verses. Even if you can't write them from memory, take the time to fill them in.

As we wrap up our study, I'm asking the Lord to take the conviction he's given, the sin he's exposed, and the encouragement he's offered, and use it to transform us all more into the image of Jesus. May we be steadfast women reflecting the beauty of our steadfast Savior.

DAY 1

PRAY

Father, thank you that you've spoken to us through your Holy Word, and for your servant, James. Thank you that your Word is true and trustworthy. Please grant me wisdom and humility as I study and apply your glorious truths. I ask this in Jesus's name. Amen.

1. James began his letter by talking about various trials and how we are to respond. What have you learned about how to remain steadfast through the trials of life?

2. James has instructed us on how to pray and how not to pray. What have you learned? How will his instruction shape your prayer life?

DAY 2

◆

PRAY

Father, thank you for giving us your Word, for telling us who you are. Thank you that you didn't leave us alone, but you've revealed yourself to us. I ask that you give me an insatiable hunger for your Word—that I would seek you, find you, know you, love you, and worship you more. I ask this in Jesus's name. Amen.

1. James emphasized the importance of our words. What has been the most convicting and why?

2. We have also learned about wisdom, both true and false. How would you summarize godly wisdom and how will you pursue it?

DAY 3

Almighty God, shine the light of your Holy Word into the recesses of
my mind and heart: illuminate and expose what I think and what I
love. Conform my thoughts and my affections to yours, Lord. I ask
this in Jesus's name. Amen.

1. James said a lot about wealth, poverty, and how we care for
    the poor. How would you summarize James's thoughts on these
    things? What, if anything, will change in your life as a result?

2. What has the Lord taught you about pride and humility? How
    has it changed you?

DAY 4

◆

PRAY

Father, Son, and Spirit, I bow before you. Thank you that you are merciful, gracious, slow to anger, and abounding in steadfast love and faithfulness. I ask that your steadfast love would steady me in the midst of my life's circumstances. I ask this in Jesus's name. Amen.

1. How would you summarize what you've learned about faith and works? How will you live differently as a result?

2. How have you grown more steadfast as a result of spending time in the book of James?

DAY 5

PRAY

Father, Son, and Holy Spirit, thank you for all the ways you've met me in the book of James. Thank you that your Word is living and active and has changed me. I ask that you not let the convictions you've given fade, the sin you've exposed remain, or the lessons you've taught be forgotten. Make me, I pray, a doer, and not a hearer only, of your Word. I ask this in Jesus's holy name. Amen.

1. We've saved the most important question of all for last. What have you learned about God by studying James? How has your love of him grown as a result?

MEMORY VERSE QUIZ:

James 1:17

James 1:22

James 2:18

James 3:10

James 4:6

James 5:11

James 5:16

CHAPTER 8

GROUP DISCUSSION QUESTIONS

◆

Spend your small group time discussing the questions from this week.

Endnotes

◆

1. Craig L. Blomberg and Mariam J. Kamell, *James: Zondervan Exegetical Commentary on the New Testament* (Grand Rapids, MI: Zondervan, 2008), 35.
2. If you find it easier to memorize by listening to the text, here are links to two websites that might be helpful. The first, http://www.streetlightsbible.com, offers a downloadable app with James read aloud over a hip hop score. The second, https://noisetrade.com/indeliblepublishing/james, offers the book of James set to percussion and song.
3. Daniel M. Doriani, *James* (Phillipsburg, NJ: P & R Pub., 2007), 16.
4. Douglas J. Moo, *The Letter of James* (Grand Rapids: William B. Eerdmans Publishing Company, 2016), 81.
5. Five scholars agree that James was most likely the first book of the New Testament written.
6. Blomberg and Kamell, James, 106.
7. Moo, *The Letter of James*, 90.
8. Doriani, *James*, 61.
9. Moo, *The Letter of James*, 118.
10. J.A. Motyer, *The Message of James* (Downers Grove, IL.: Intervarsity Press, 1985), 109.
11. Doriani, *James*, 95.
12. I was helped greatly by Robert Peterson's work on this topic. Robert A. Peterson, *Salvation Accomplished by the Son: The Work of Christ* (Wheaton, IL: Crossway, 2012).
13. Drawings by Rebecca Doctor, 2019.
14. Motyer, *The Message of James*, 134.
15. Ibid, 151.
16. John Piper, *Desiring God: Meditations of a Christian Hedonist* (CO Springs, CO: Multnomah Books, 2017), 10.
17. Rick Warren, *The Purpose Driven Life* (Grand Rapids, MI: Zondervan, 2002), 148.
18. Steve Bateman, "@SteveBatemanFBC," Twitter, May 2019, https://twitter.com/SteveBatemanFBC.

19. Jessica Hanson, "20 Most Popular Funeral Songs," Avalon Funeral Plans, September 11, 2017, https://www.avalonfuneralplans.com/blog/20-best-funeral-songs/.

20. Motyer, *The Message of James*, 161.

21. Ibid, 169.

22. Ibid, 161.

23. Douglas J. Moo, *The Epistle of James: An Introduction and Commentary*, (Grand Rapids, MI: Eerdmans, 2002), 230.

24. Doriani, *James*, 197.

25. Motyer, *The Message of James*, 199.

26. Doriani, *James*, 194.

27. Ibid, 200.

.

TGC THE GOSPEL COALITION

THE GOSPEL COALITION is a fellowship of evangelical churches deeply committed to renewing our faith in the gospel of Christ and to reforming our ministry practices to conform fully to the Scriptures. We have committed ourselves to invigorating churches with new hope and compelling joy based on the promises received by grace alone through faith alone in Christ alone.

We desire to champion the gospel with clarity, compassion, courage, and joy—gladly linking hearts with fellow believers across denominational, ethnic, and class lines. We yearn to work with all who, in addition to embracing our confession and theological vision for ministry, seek the lordship of Christ over the whole of life with unabashed hope in the power of the Holy Spirit to transform individuals, communities, and cultures.

Through its women's initiatives, The Gospel Coalition aims to support the growth of women in faithfully studying and sharing the Scriptures; in actively loving and serving the church; and in spreading the gospel of Jesus Christ in all their callings.

Join the cause and visit TGC.org for fresh resources that will equip you to love God with all your heart, soul, mind, and strength, and to love your neighbor as yourself.

tgc.org

Also available from
The Gospel Coalition

•

Made in the USA
Columbia, SC
18 January 2024

30616086R00137